BACKYARD
SCIENCE &
DISCOVERY
WORKBOOK

MIDWEST

ADVENTURE PUBLICATIONS

TABLE OF CONTENTS

ABOUT THIS BOOK

The Midwest is a wonderful place. With 12 states, four distinct seasons, and a huge range of habitats, plants, animals, and fungi, there's an amazing amount to observe and learn about. Over the past decade, I've been lucky enough to serve as the editor of several hundred books about the Midwest, many of them field guides to birds, rocks and minerals, insects, mushrooms, or other topics about the natural world.

I love what I do at work because it's what I do at home. When I'm not working, I'm usually outside: hiking, taking photographs of animals, plants, or mushrooms, or doing science projects with my kids.

My goal with this workbook is simple: I want to help get kids outside and observing nature in the Midwest, so they can learn to love and protect it. Once you start looking, there's so much to appreciate and observe, even in a backyard or a nearby park.

This book features **18 hands-on science projects,** such as raising native caterpillars, making mushroom spore prints, and attracting moths and other insects with an ultraviolet light; **more than 20 simple, fun introductions** to the region's habitats, birds, seasons, and rocks and minerals; and **more than a dozen fun activities** to help you make hypotheses, observe nature, and learn about the world around you.

That's really the fun part: you really never know what you're going to find on any given day. It's a little like a treasure hunt, and if you keep good records and share what you find, your observations can even help scientists learn more about the world (or help you start off a career as a scientist).

So get outside, have fun, and share your discoveries!

Brett Ortler

GEOGRAPHY OF THE MIDWEST

Also known as the Heartland, the Midwest includes 12 states and spans a pretty huge area. Practice your geography and label the states below. Bonus points if you can name the capitals of each.

Answers on page 136!

IL _____

IN _____

IA _____

KS _____

MI _____

MN _____

MO _____

NE _____

ND _____

OH _____

SD _____

WI _____

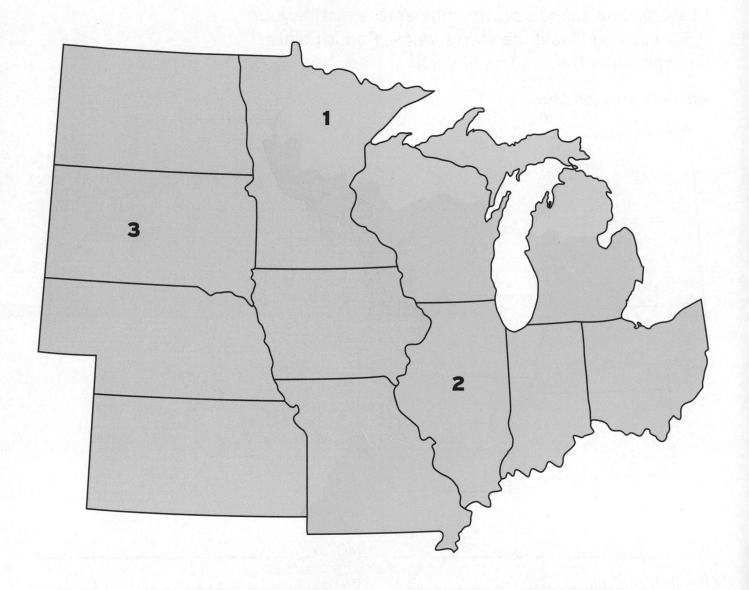

GET TO KNOW THE MIDWEST'S BIOMES

The best way to get to know your Midwestern state—and your backyard—is by understanding the natural neighborhood it belongs to in the Midwest: its biome. A **biome** is a community of animals and plants that live in a specific kind of climate and environment.

You've probably heard of some biomes before: grasslands, forests, and so on.

The Midwest is home to several different biomes:

1. Coniferous Forests

2. Temperate Forests

3. Grasslands

QUICK QUIZ

1. Which **biome** do you live in?

_____

_____

_____

CONIFEROUS FORESTS

A **conifer** is a tree that has cones; while you're probably familiar with woody pine cones, there are actually two different kinds. The male cones are smaller and produce pollen that is blown by the wind. The female cones are larger, and after they are pollinated they become woody and produce seeds. Almost all conifers are **evergreen**, which means they don't lose their leaves (though some, like the tamarack, do). Not all of the trees in a coniferous forest are conifers, but many of them are.

Coniferous forests are found in the northern part of the Midwest, where it's often quite cold in the winter.

QUICK QUIZ

Which of the following trees is **evergreen**?

A. Tamarack

B. Eastern
White Pine

C. Maple

D. Oak

Answer on page 136!

1. Make a list of the evergreen trees near you.

_____

_____

_____

_____

2. What deciduous trees (trees that lose their leaves)
   are nearby?

_____

_____

_____

_____

TEMPERATE FORESTS

The word **temperate** means mild or moderate; in temperate forests, there are long periods (summer!) where the weather is warm. These forests primarily have **deciduous** trees (trees that lose their leaves), such as maples, oaks, and basswood, though conifers can grow (or be planted) there as well. Temperate forests are home to familiar creatures, such as raccoons, woodpeckers, and White-Tailed Deer, but they also have thousands upon thousands of species of insects, fungi, and plants.

QUICK QUIZ

There are many different kinds of trees in the Midwest's deciduous forests, but maples, oaks, and basswoods are very common.

Can you identify each tree's leaves?

1. _____ 2. _____ 3. _____

Answers on page 136!

1. How many different deciduous trees can you find near you?

_____

_____

_____

_____

2. Which one is your favorite? Why?

_____

_____

_____

_____

GRASSLANDS

The **grasslands**, or prairies, once spanned across huge portions of the Midwest. Tallgrass prairies are home to plants like Big Bluestem that grow to incredible heights—almost 10 feet tall in some cases—and their hard, tough roots grow deep into the soil. Further west, shortgrass prairies and mixed-grass prairies covered even more of the land. European settlers initially viewed the prairies as wastelands and immediately set about converting the land, and its valuable soil, to farmland. Today, only a tiny fraction of the prairie remains, and many of the animals and plants that depended on the prairie have been **extirpated**.

QUICK QUIZ

In the sentence, "Many of the animals and plants that depended on the prairie have been extirpated," the word **extirpated** means:

A. Saved or protected

B. Moved to another area

C. Wiped out of their original habitat

D. All have been sent to zoos

Answer on page 136!

1. What other animals in your state are endangered or have been extirpated?

_____

_____

_____

_____

_____

_____

_____

_____

_____

_____

THEN VS. NOW

European settlement changed the biomes of the Midwest a great deal. Nearly all of the original prairie was converted to farmland, and clear-cutting of the forests was complete by the early 1920s. These intentional changes upended the ecosystems of the region, reducing or eliminating populations of iconic animals such as bison, elk, and beaver, which were important (or essential) to the traditional lifestyles of the Indigenous peoples of the Midwest.

A farm site being cleared in the forests of northern Minnesota.

QUICK QUIZ

Which animals used to be common in large parts of the Midwest but are now rare or absent altogether?

A. Bison

B. Prairie Dog

C. Elk

D. Passenger Pigeon

E. All of them

Answer on page 136!

Prairie Dog

STATE SYMBOLS

Another good way to get to know the region is by learning which plants, animals, and natural materials are your state's official symbols. From the state bird and flower, which you might know already, to lesser-known categories, such as state amphibian, gemstone, or fossil, these symbols are usually selected because they have a long history with the state. Not every state has the same categories or names for state symbols, but they are still a good way to learn about your state and its wildlife.

QUICK QUIZ

There are five state symbols on the following pages that aren't actually found naturally in that state (**native**), or even in North America.

Which one of the following five plants or animals is actually **native** to the U.S.?

A. Honeybee (Insect of Wisconsin, South Dakota, Missouri, Nebraska, and Kansas)

B. Norway Pine (Tree of Minnesota)

C. Ring-Necked Pheasant (Bird of South Dakota)

D. Red Carnation (Flower of Ohio)

E. Peony (Flower of Indiana)

F. Missouri Mule (Animal of Missouri)

Answer on page 136!

ILLINOIS

Eastern Tiger Salamander

Amphibian

Painted Turtle

Reptile

Violet

Flower

White Oak

Tree

Northern Cardinal

Bird

Monarch Butterfly

Insect

Bluegill

Fish

Fluorite

Mineral

White-Tailed Deer

Animal

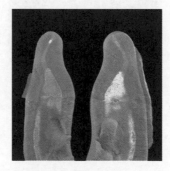

Tully Monster

Fossil

STATE SYMBOLS

INDIANA

Peony

Flower

Tulip Tree

Tree

Salem Limestone

Stone

Northern Cardinal

Bird

IOWA

American Goldfinch

Bird

Wild Prairie Rose

Flower

Geode

Rock

Oak

Tree

KANSAS

Native Sunflower

Flower

Western Meadowlark

Bird

American Buffalo (Bison)

Animal

Honeybee

Insect

Ornate Box Turtle

Reptile

Barred Tiger Salamander

Amphibian

Greenhorn Limestone

Rock

Galena

Mineral

Channel Catfish

Fish

STATE SYMBOLS

MICHIGAN

American Robin

Bird

Brook Trout

Fish

Apple Blossom

Flower

Mastodon

Fossil

White-Tailed Deer

Mammal

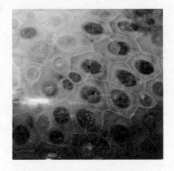

Petoskey Stone

Stone

Western Painted Turtle

Reptile

Isle Royale Greenstone

Gem

Eastern White Pine

Tree

Dwarf Lake Iris

Wildflower

MINNESOTA

Common Loon

Bird

Pink Lady's Slipper

Flower

Lake Superior Agate

Gemstone

Norway Pine

Tree

Walleye

Fish

Monarch Butterfly

Butterfly

Rusty Patched Bumblebee

Bee

STATE SYMBOLS

MISSOURI

Missouri Mule

Animal

Eastern Bluebird

Bird

Crinoid

Fossil

Honeybee

Insect

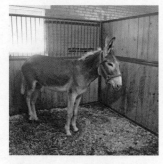

Galena

Mineral

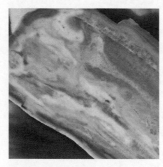

Mozarkite

Rock

Channel Catfish

Fish

Flowering Dogwood

Tree

American Bullfrog

Amphibian

Crayfish

Invertebrate

Three-Toed Box Turtle

Reptile

NEBRASKA

Western Meadowlark

Bird

Goldenrod

Flower

Blue Chalcedony

Gem

Eastern Cottonwood

Tree

Mammoth

Fossil

Prairie Agate

Rock

White-Tailed Deer

Mammal

Honeybee

Insect

Channel Catfish

Fish

STATE SYMBOLS

NORTH DAKOTA

Western Meadowlark

Bird

Wild Prairie Rose

Flower

Teredo Petrified Wood

Fossil

American Elm

Tree

Northern Pike

Fish

Convergent Lady Beetle

Insect

1. If *you* could choose state symbols for your state, what would you pick?

_____

_____

_____

_____

OHIO

Red Carnation
Flower

Northern Cardinal
Bird

Buckeye
Tree

Ohio Flint
Gemstone

Ladybug
Insect

***Isotelus* (Trilobite)**
Fossil

White-Tailed Deer
Mammal

Black Racer Snake
Reptile

Pawpaw
Native Fruit

American Bullfrog
Frog

STATE SYMBOLS

SOUTH DAKOTA

Ring-Necked Pheasant

Bird

American Pasque Flower

Flower

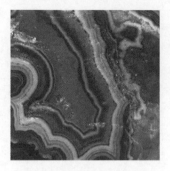

Fairburn Agate

Gemstone

Rose Quartz

Mineral

Black Hills Spruce

Tree

Triceratops

Fossil

Honeybee

Insect

Coyote

Animal

Walleye

Fish

WISCONSIN

American Robin
Bird

Wood Violet
Flower

Granite
Stone

Galena
Mineral

Calymene celebra
(Trilobite)
Fossil

Sugar Maple
Tree

Badger
Animal

White-Tailed Deer
Wildlife Animal

Muskellunge
Fish

Honeybee
Insect

INTRODUCED VS. INVASIVE

Over the course of settlement of the Midwest, many plants and animals were **introduced** to the region. Some of these, such as soybeans or horses, were introduced on purpose; they are **nonnative** but haven't been a problem. Others were introduced either on purpose or by accident, and once they got here they spread quickly, often finding an environment with few predators. These species then became **invasive**, spreading uncontrollably and hurting native animals and plants.

A few familiar, but invasive, species:

Canada Thistle

Most Earthworms

Garlic Mustard

German Carp

Glossy Buckthorn

House Sparrow

Starling

QUICK QUIZ

Which of the following animals is an introduced species in the Midwest?

A. Northern
   Cardinal

B. Northern Pike

C. Cow

D. Monarch
   Butterfly

Answer on page 136!

1. Can you think of other introduced species in your area?
   Hint: Most farm animals aren't from here! The same is true
   for many weeds.

_____

_____

_____

_____

_____

_____

_____

_____

_____

GETTING TO KNOW
YOUR WEATHER

You probably know what a hot summer day is like, but what's the hottest you remember? Ninety degrees, maybe 100? What do you think the highest temperature recorded anywhere in your state was? **Note:** It probably didn't reach this temperature in the place you live, but it did happen *somewhere* in your state.

MAKE A HYPOTHESIS

1. Highest maximum temperature in my state?

_____

_____

2. OK, and you've felt cold, too, maybe shivering at the bus stop or walking to school. So what do you think the coldest temperature recorded anywhere in your state is?

_____

_____

3. And do you like making snow forts or having snowball fights? Me too. But what do you think the maximum amount of snow on the ground—anywhere in your state—was? A foot? Two? More?

_____

_____

A FEW MIDWEST WEATHER RECORDS

STATE NAME	HIGHEST TEMP (°F)	LOWEST TEMP (°F)	DEEPEST SNOW (INCHES)
Illinois	117° (1954)	-38° (2019)	41" (1979)
Indiana	116° (1936)	-36° (1994)	47" (1918)
Iowa	118° (1934)	-47° (1996)	52" (1969)
Kansas	121° (1936)	-40° (1905)	40" (1918)
Michigan	112° (1936)	-51° (1934)	117" (1948)
Minnesota	115° (1917)	-60° (1996)	88" (1969)
Missouri	118° (1954)	-40° (1905)	36" (1960)
Nebraska	118° (1934)	-47° (1899)	44" (1936)
North Dakota	121° (1936)	-60° (1936)	65" (1897)
Ohio	113° (1934)	-39° (1899)	47" (1996)
South Dakota	120° (2006)	-58° (1936)	73" (1998)
Wisconsin	114° (1936)	-55° (1996)	83" (1933)

Source: ncdc.noaa.gov/extremes/scec/records

IS THE SUN SETTING EARLIER?!

In winter, you've probably noticed how it gets darker earlier. That happens because Earth is tilted on its axis, so certain parts of the planet get more daylight in some seasons than in others. If you've traveled to the north or to the south of where you live, you've probably noticed that the amount of daylight varies with **latitude** (how far north or south you are from the equator).

MAKE A HYPOTHESIS

1. What month do you think has the shortest day of the year in the Midwest?

_____

2. Which month has the longest day of the year in the Midwest?

_____

3. On the shortest day of the year where you live, what time is sunset?

_____

LONGEST & SHORTEST DAYS
ACROSS THE MIDWEST

The longest day of the year in the Midwest is known as the **summer solstice**. That's when the North Pole has its maximum tilt toward the sun. The shortest day in the Midwest is known as the **winter solstice**, when the North Pole is tilted away the most from the sun.

The date that each solstice occurs varies a little each year, but the summer solstice in the northern hemisphere always occurs between June 20 and June 22, and the winter solstice always occurs between December 20 and December 23.

In an upcoming solstice, I've listed when the sun will set in several places across the Midwest. The first is in the far north; the second is roughly in the middle of the region, and the third locale is in the far southern portion of the region.

In southern Missouri, on the winter solstice, the sun rises about 40 minutes earlier than in Minnesota, and the sun stays out about 40 minutes longer!

WINTER SOLSTICE

N. Minnesota (International Falls)
December 21
Sunrise: 8:03 am
Sunset: 4:20 pm

Central Iowa (Des Moines)
December 21
Sunrise: 7:00 am
Sunset: 5:55 pm

S. Missouri (Branson)
December 21
Sunrise: 7:21 am
Sunset: 5:00 pm

SUMMER SOLSTICE

N. Minnesota (International Falls)
June 20
Sunrise: 5:17 am
Sunset: 9:26 pm

Central Iowa (Des Moines)
June 20
Sunrise: 5:40 am
Sunset: 8:51 pm

S. Missouri (Branson)
June 20
Sunrise: 5:54 am
Sunset: 8:34 pm

Source: esrl.noaa.gov/gmd/grad/solcalc

AVERAGE LAST FROST DATES

Anxious to plant your garden? Well, before you get out and start planting, you have to keep the temperature in mind. If it gets too cold outside (especially overnight), the water within the plants will freeze, and the plants will be damaged, or die altogether (this is called a killing frost). This is one reason why gardeners wait until the danger of a frost has passed.

Here are the approximate dates of the last spring frosts across the Midwest:

- **Southern Minnesota, Wisconsin, and portions of the Dakotas:** first two weeks of May

- **Northern Minnesota, Wisconsin, Michigan and North Dakota:** last two weeks of May

- **Central Midwest, which include Iowa and Illinois:** last two weeks of April

- **Southern Missouri:** first two weeks of April

By the way, frost is one of the most interesting things to photograph in the winter:

GET TO KNOW THE SEASONS & THE WEATHER

The seasons of the year are like the hours on a clock: winter is the night, spring is the morning, summer is the afternoon, and fall is twilight. If you pay attention to this seasonal clock, and the animals and plants found during each season, you'll be studying **phenology**. That's the study of the cycles of the seasons and the natural world over time. By studying the phenology of your area—when certain birds arrive in spring, or when raspberries are first ripe in summer, or when the first inch of snow falls—you'll learn a lot about the natural world around you and what to expect next.

START OUT BY MAKING SOME PREDICTIONS

Before you start observing, see what you already know. Make some predictions about when you expect to see the wildlife around you. You might not have seen all of these animals or plants before. If not, that's OK, but make predictions about those you recognize.

Robins don't always migrate away during the winter, but they definitely are easier to spot during some months of the year.

1. What season do you notice robins in the most?

_____

_____

2. In which month?

_____

_____

American Robin

3. In which month do lilacs bloom where you live?

_____

_____

4. In which month(s) do the trees get their leaves where you live?

_____

_____

Lilacs

5. When do they lose them?

_____

6. When are raspberries ripe where you live?

_____

7. Strawberries?

_____

Raspberries

8. In which month(s) do you see Monarch Butterflies?

_____

_____

9. Do you have apple trees or crabapples nearby? In which season can you harvest apples?

_____

_____

Wild Strawberries

10. When does it normally snow where you live?

_____

11. Which months does it never or rarely snow where you live?

_____

Monarch Butterfly

DO-IT-YOURSELF PHENOLOGY

The easiest way to start out with phenology is by observing one type of plant or animal throughout the year. Try this with the plants or animals near you. For example, if you have a maple tree or an oak nearby, keep track of when it loses it leaves, and then, in the spring, when the buds emerge, flowers and leaves form, and when fruit (seeds or acorns) develops. Jot down a few notes about the weather over the past few days, too, as rain, temperature are often the drivers of natural phenomena.

For example, you might want to keep track of things like:

Date: _____ / _____ / _____

Buds form: _____

Flowers form: _____

Leaves emerge: _____

Seeds form: _____

Tree is fully "leafed out": _____

Leaves change colors in fall: _____

Leaves start falling off tree: _____

Then, keep track of that same tree the next year, and see how different those same dates are. Does the tree have buds the same day of each year? How about seeds? What was the weather like?

Date: _____ /_____ /_____

Buds form: _____

Flowers form: _____

Leaves emerge: _____

Seeds form:_____

Tree is fully "leafed out":_____

Leaves change colors in fall:_____

Leaves start falling off tree: _____

Maple leaves in fall

PHENOLOGY CALENDAR: SPRING

Certain natural events tend to happen around the same time each year. Such events can vary each year, especially by location, so keeping track of when you spot plants, animals, and natural events is a great way to really get to know nature in your area.

MARCH

- Skunk Cabbage, a plant that can generate its own heat to melt snow, emerges; it's found in the eastern Midwest
- American Robins are really starting to be noticeable
- Red-Winged Blackbirds arrive
- Bluebirds arrive
- Lakes begin losing their ice in more-southern portions of the Midwest (this is called **ice-out**)

What I spotted in March:

Red-Winged Blackbird

Skunk Cabbage

_____

_____

_____

_____

_____

_____

_____

APRIL

- Most lakes in the northern part of the region lose their ice
- Dandelions grow, then flower
- Loons return to the lakes
- Robins are building nests
- Bumblebees start visiting flowers
- Dark-Eyed Juncos are migrating out of our area
- Eastern Bluebirds begin making nests
- Mallards are active
- Painted Turtles begin to be visible
- Many maple trees are producing **samaras** (also known as **helicopter seeds**)

What I spotted in April:

_____

_____

_____

_____

_____

_____

_____

_____

_____

_____

Robin's nest

Sugar Maple flower

Dandelion

Eastern Bluebird

Source for all phenology data: www.usanpn.org/data

MAY

- Lilacs are blooming
- Adult Mourning Cloak butterflies are active
- Luna Moths appear in the north; they may be visible earlier farther south
- Monarch Butterflies are active
- Baltimore Orioles return
- Bullfrogs are calling
- Milkweed has leaves
- Hummingbirds are active
- Plum trees are flowering
- American Goldfinches are building their nests
- Morel Mushrooms appear in the northern part of the region in May, earlier in the south.
- Mayfly hatches start; some include so many insects they can be seen on weather radar

Lilac

Mourning Cloak

Luna Moth

Baltimore Oriole

Morel Mushroom

What I spotted in May:

_____

_____

_____

_____

_____

_____

_____

_____

PHENOLOGY CALENDAR: SUMMER

JUNE

- Monarch Butterfly adults are active
- Wild strawberries are ripe
- Fireflies are visible in much of the Midwest
- Dragonfly adults emerge, and you can sometimes see dozens at a time
- Adult June bugs emerge, though they can often be seen in May or into July

What I spotted in June:

Monarch Butterfly

Wild Strawberries

Firefly

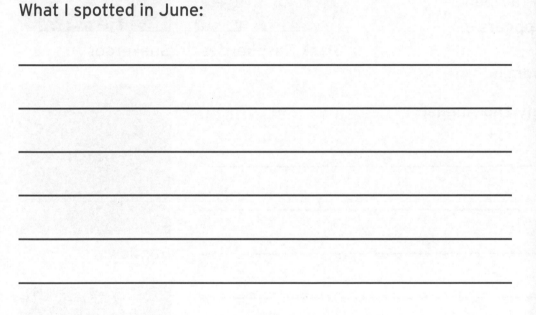

JULY

- Chokecherry fruits are ripe
- Many prairie wildflowers bloom
- Adult Dog-Day Cicadas are singing; you'll find the papery exoskeletons they leave behind too
- Black Raspberries and blueberries are ripe

Dog-Day Cicada

Soybeans

AUGUST

- Soybeans in field start turning yellow in late August
- Black cherry fruit is ripe
- Plums are starting to ripen
- White Snakeroot appears in late August
- Sunflowers are blooming

What I spotted in July and August:

_____

_____

_____

_____

_____

_____

_____

_____

Black Raspberries

Snakeroot

Sunflowers

Blueberries

PHENOLOGY CALENDAR: FALL

SEPTEMBER

- Ripe Jack in the Pulpit berries are visible (don't eat them; they're toxic!)
- Sumac leaves are turning red
- Poison Ivy leaves turn yellow or red (don't touch!)
- Goldenrod flowers are visible everywhere, often along roadsides
- Hazelnut fruits are ripe
- Tamarack needles start turning orange
- Bears are entering their winter dens
- Acorns start dropping from oaks
- Gray squirrels are busy caching (storing) acorns for winter

What I spotted in September:

_____

_____

_____

_____

_____

_____

_____

Jack in the Pulpit

Sumac

Tamarack

Poison Ivy

OCTOBER

- Dark-Eyed Juncos begin to arrive
- Tamarack needles fall off

NOVEMBER

- First snow usually falls in much of the region
- Most migrating birds have long since left

What I spotted in October and November:

Dark-Eyed Junco

Migrating Sandhill Cranes

Snowfall

PHENOLOGY CALENDAR: WINTER

DECEMBER

- First snow usually falls in southern portions of the Midwest; this is a good time to start looking for animal tracks!

JANUARY

- Lakes are covered in ice in most places
- January is the snowiest month for much of the Midwest (though in some areas it's December); it's also the coldest month throughout the Midwest

FEBRUARY

- Maple sap begins running
- Bald Eagles are nesting

What I spotted in the winter:

_____

_____

_____

_____

_____

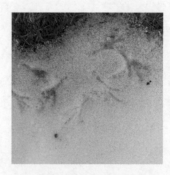
Bird tracks in the snow

Ice fishing

Maple sap

Bald Eagle

YOUR STATE'S MAJOR FARM CROPS & FARM PRODUCTS

After settlement, much of the Midwest became farmland. A wide variety of crops are grown in the Midwest. Apples and cherries are grown in places like Michigan, and the region is home to corn and soybean powerhouses such as Iowa, Nebraska, and Minnesota. These are the top crops, or **commodities (agricultural products)**, in the Midwest.

ILLINOIS

- Corn
- Soybeans
- Hogs
- Cattle
- Other

INDIANA

- Corn
- Soybeans
- Hogs
- Dairy Products/Milk
- Chicken Eggs

IOWA

- Corn
- Hogs
- Soybeans
- Cattle
- Dairy Products/Milk

KANSAS

- Cattle
- Corn
- Soybeans
- Wheat
- Sorghum

MICHIGAN

- Milk
- Corn
- Soybeans
- Cattle
- Other

MINNESOTA

- Soybeans
- Corn
- Hogs
- Feed
- Other

MISSOURI

- Soybeans
- Cattle
- Corn
- Hogs
- Chicken

NEBRASKA

- Cattle
- Corn
- Soybeans
- Hogs
- Dairy Products/Milk

NORTH DAKOTA

- Soybeans
- Wheat
- Corn
- Cattle
- Canola

OHIO

- Soybeans
- Corn
- Milk
- Hogs
- Cattle

SOUTH DAKOTA

- Cattle
- Corn
- Soybeans
- Hogs
- Dairy Products/Milk

WISCONSIN

- Dairy Products/Milk
- Cattle
- Corn
- Soybeans

QUICK QUIZ

If you haven't lived near a farm or worked on one, you might not recognize the crops growing in the field. Can you identify each type of crop?

1. _____   2. _____   3. _____   4. _____

Answers on page 136!

WHAT'S THE HIGHEST & LOWEST POINT IN YOUR STATE?

The Midwest isn't exactly known for being a land of towering mountains or dramatic ravines, but it isn't just the flat farm country you might think. When measuring a state's elevation, or that of a mountain or a hill, geographers compare a given place's elevation with that of sea level. So for example, Florida's highest point—in the entire state—is only 345 feet above sea level. That's not exactly surprising, since it's surrounded by ocean.

What do you think the highest point is in your state? What about the lowest?

Highest: _____ feet above sea level

Lowest: _____ feet above sea level

FAST FACT

Visiting the highest point in an area is something of a growing hobby. Known as **highpointing,** this is a fun way to get to know your state, and its quirks, a little better. Though in some places, such as Alaska, where the highest point is 20,310 feet, you'll definitely need a lot of experience, gear, and training before you ever make an attempt.

Source: www.usgs.gov/science-support/osqi/yes/resources-teachers/highest-and-lowest-elevations

ILLINOIS

Highest Point Above Sea Level:	Lowest Point Above Sea Level:
1,235 feet	**279 feet**
Charles Mound, Jo Daviess County	*Mississippi River, Alexander County*

INDIANA

Highest Point Above Sea Level:	Lowest Point Above Sea Level:
1,257 feet	**320 feet**
Hoosier Hill, Wayne County	*Ohio River, Posey County*

IOWA

Highest Point Above Sea Level:	Lowest Point Above Sea Level:
1,670 feet	**480 feet**
Hawkeye Point, Osceola County	*Mississippi River, Lee County*

KANSAS

Highest Point Above Sea Level:	Lowest Point Above Sea Level:
4,039 feet	**679 feet**
Mount Sunflower, Wallace County	*Verdigris River, Montgomery County*

*highest locations shown for each state

HIGHEST & LOWEST POINTS

MICHIGAN

Highest Point Above Sea Level:

1,979 feet
Mount Arvon, Baraga County

Lowest Point Above Sea Level:

571 feet
Lake Erie

MINNESOTA

Highest Point Above Sea Level:

2,301 feet
Eagle Mountain, Cook County

Lowest Point Above Sea Level:

601 feet
Lake Superior

MISSOURI

Highest Point Above Sea Level:

1,772 feet
Taum Sauk Mountain, Iron County

Lowest Point Above Sea Level:

230 feet
Saint Francis River, Dunklin County

NEBRASKA

Highest Point Above Sea Level:

5,424 feet
Panorama Point, Kimball County

Lowest Point Above Sea Level:

479 feet
Missouri River, Richardson County

*highest locations shown for each state

NORTH DAKOTA

Highest Point Above Sea Level:

3,506 feet
*White Butte,
Slope County*

Lowest Point Above Sea Level:

750 feet
*Red River of the North,
Pembina County*

OHIO

Highest Point Above Sea Level:

1,550 feet
*Campbell Hill,
Logan County*

Lowest Point Above Sea Level:

455 feet
*Ohio River,
Hamilton County*

SOUTH DAKOTA

Highest Point Above Sea Level:

7,242 feet
*Black Elk Peak,
Pennington County*

Lowest Point Above Sea Level:

966 feet
*Big Stone Lake,
Roberts County*

WISCONSIN

Highest Point Above Sea Level:

1,951 feet
*Timms Hill,
Price County*

Lowest Point Above Sea Level:

579 feet
Lake Michigan

*highest locations shown for each state

SPOT YOUR STATE BIRD

AMERICAN GOLDFINCH

State Bird of Iowa

WHEN WILL I SEE THEM?
Found year-round in much of the Midwest, and during the summer in the Dakotas and the northwestern parts of Minnesota and Nebraska, the bright-yellow males (and somewhat drabber females) come to seed feeders in backyards.

WILL THEY COME TO MY YARD?
Yes! Goldfinches eat seeds, and they aren't exactly picky about what kind, though they love sunflower seeds and nyjer seed (which is often sold in ready-made "socks" to hang outside).

AMERICAN ROBIN

State Bird of Wisconsin and Michigan

WHEN WILL I SEE THEM?
Robins are most obvious in spring through fall, when they are easy to spot hopping around yards, with their heads tipped to the side, looking for worms and bugs. But in all but the northernmost parts of the Midwest (North Dakota, northern Minnesota, the Upper Peninsula of Michigan, and parts of Wisconsin), they often stick around during the winter, although they aren't as obvious. That's because they have to resort to other food sources, such as fruit still clinging to winter trees. On cold days, you can sometimes see them fluffed up in trees, looking pretty unhappy as they try to stay warm.

WILL THEY COME TO MY YARD?
Robins don't come to birdseed feeders, but they will sometimes come to suet (animal fat) feeders. If you really want to attract them, leave out fruit or mealworms.

COMMON LOON

State Bird of Minnesota

WHEN WILL I SEE THEM?

Common Loons in the Midwest spend the winters near the Gulf of Mexico, but in summer, they breed on lakes in the northern parts of the region, especially Minnesota, Wisconsin, and Michigan, and way up into Canada as well. During migration season (spring, fall) you might see one. And if you haven't ever heard one, look up its call. It's hauntingly beautiful and part of the background of summer in the far north.

WILL THEY COME TO MY YARD?

Nope! Loons nest on large lakes. They walk poorly on land, and they need a certain amount of water to take off. But if you happen to visit a cabin in the northern parts of the Midwest, you may well hear or see one. If a lake is large enough, it can have several different loon pairs on it.

EASTERN BLUEBIRD

State Bird of Missouri

WHEN WILL I SEE THEM?

Bluebirds are found in the northern parts of the Midwest in the summer, and year-round in the rest of the Midwest, so there's a very good chance you can spot one! The male is a bright sky blue and a rusty red on its chest. The female is less blue and lighter brown.

WILL THEY COME TO MY YARD?

These birds don't come to seed feeders, but they love to eat mealworms, so if you put some wiggly mealworms in a dish, they might show up. The best way to get them to visit is to put up a nesting box for them. Bluebirds are cavity nesters in nature: they nest in cavities (holes) in dead trees. But natural cavities have become rarer because of human development (and invasive species), so putting up a nest box will help out bluebirds and give you a good chance to have a bright blue visitor!

SPOT YOUR STATE BIRD

NORTHERN CARDINAL

State Bird of Ohio, Indiana, and Illinois

WHEN WILL I SEE THEM?

This beautiful bird is found year-round throughout much of the Midwest, but it isn't found in most of the Dakotas or northern Minnesota. The males are a brilliant red, similar to the color of the garments of cardinals, officials who help lead the Roman Catholic Church (that's why these birds are called cardinals). The females are equally pretty but are more of a subdued brown, with some red accents on the wings and tail.

WILL THEY COME TO MY YARD?

Cardinals, like many other birds, love black oil sunflower seeds, among other kinds. They are especially fun to see in the winter, when their bright colors contrast nicely with falling snow.

RING-NECKED PHEASANT

State Bird of South Dakota

WHEN WILL I SEE THEM?

This bird actually isn't native to the United States, or even to North America. Native to Asia, it has been a popular game bird (a bird hunted for meat and sport) almost everywhere it's been introduced, including across much of the Midwest, where it's now often a common sight and a popular hunting target.

WILL THEY COME TO MY YARD?

These big, colorful birds might visit your yard if you leave out cracked corn on the ground.

WESTERN MEADOWLARK

State Bird of North Dakota, Nebraska, and Kansas

WHEN WILL I SEE THEM?
As its name suggests, the Western Meadowlark is found in the western part of the Midwest. It's not found often in Ohio and Indiana, but it breeds in the Dakotas east into Michigan. It's found year-round farther south in the Midwest and in wintering populations there too.

WILL THEY COME TO MY YARD?
These prairie-loving birds like open spaces, and in their breeding range they might visit a birdhouse or a seed feeder.

1. Have you spotted your state bird? Where?

_____

_____

_____

2. What's your favorite state bird in the Midwest?

_____

_____

_____

3. How about your favorite bird in your state?

_____

_____

_____

MAKE YOUR YARD BIRD-FRIENDLY

Lawns are pretty, but they don't do a lot to help birds, bugs, and most other kinds of wildlife. To really draw birds (and the insects they often eat!) to your yard, you and your parents can make your yard a bit wilder. It's pretty easy to start doing this. Here are a few tips:

PLANT NATIVE PLANTS

Whether you're planting native trees that provide cover, nesting sites, or fruiwns to birds. For a list of what to plant, visit www.audubon.org/native-plants. To make sure you're finding the best native plants, look for a native-plant nursery near where you live.

PUT OUT A WATER SOURCE

Birds don't just need food—they need water too! A bird bath, especially one with a "water wiggler" (available at many birding or home improvement stores), is a great option. The movement of the water prevents mosquitoes from laying eggs in the water, and the sound of the moving water draws in birds from all over.

DON'T SPRAY YOUR YARD WITH BUG OR WEED KILLERS

Mosquitoes are really annoying, but the popular foggers or sprays that many people apply to their yards don't just kill mosquitoes. These insecticides often kill any bugs they touch, including bees, butterflies, and the many beetles and other creepy-crawlies that birds depend on for food. Pesticides and herbicides (weed killers) can also directly hurt birds.

Wild Geranium

Butterflyweed

Cardinal Flower

Birdbath

LEAVE OUT NEST-MAKING MATERIALS IN SPRING

Bird nests are pretty incredible, and it's even more impressive that birds make them using only their feet and their beaks!

WHAT TO DO

You can help them out by leaving natural, pesticide-free nesting materials in handy locations around your yard. Examples include soft, fluffy plant parts, such as the down from cattails, moss, or feathers you find on the ground (but make sure to wear gloves when picking those up). You can put these in easy-to-access places around your yard; on the ground, wedged into tree bark—or even hanging in an empty suet feeder.

Important Note: There are some things you don't want to give birds, especially synthetic (man-made) materials such as plastic, metal, or lint. These can be toxic to birds, either if they eat some of these things or if they absorb some of the chemicals in them.

Cattail fluff is often used in bird nests.

MAKE A RECIPE TO FEED TO BIRDS

If you get creative, you can feed birds a lot more than birdseed! Making your own bird food is a fun way to attract the birds you want to see.

Here are two options, although there are lots of others.

DO-IT-YOURSELF BIRDSEED MIX

A lot of the birdseed mixes sold in stores just aren't very good. Often, they contain lots of filler seeds (such as milo, a small, brown, round seed). Filler seeds don't have a lot of the nutrients that birds need, unlike seeds such as black oil sunflower seeds, which are full of good stuff like protein, vitamins, and fats.

So what do you do? Make your own birdseed mix! Buy some black oil sunflower seeds to use as your base, then add other seeds to those.

Here's a mix that works great for platform feeders. All of the ingredients are usually available at garden centers or home improvement stores.

WHAT YOU'LL NEED

- 4 cups black oil sunflower seeds

- 1 cup peanut chips

- 1 cup cracked corn

WHAT TO DO

Mix it all together and place it on a hanging bird feeder. For an extra-tasty treat, you can also add in some sliced apples or plums.

A SIMPLE PEANUT BUTTER BIRDSEED FEEDER

WHAT YOU'LL NEED

• Pine cones

• Peanut butter

• Black oil sunflower seeds or
  a birdseed mix

• Some string

WHAT TO DO

This tried-and-true recipe really works.
First, you'll need to collect some pine
cones. Then mix some peanut butter and
sunflower seeds in a bowl. Next, take
the pine cones and push them into the
peanut butter and seeds, making sure
everything is mixed together well like in
the picture. Now tie some string to the
top of each pine cone, and hang it from
a tree. You can do this as many times as
you like.

If you can't find any pine cones, just mix
the ingredients together, then "paint" or
smear the mixture onto a tree's bark.

1. Make both kinds of feeders, then keep track of the birds
   that come to each one! Did different birds come to the
   different feeders?

_____

_____

_____

_____

DO A BACKYARD BIRD COUNT

If you're new to birding, chances are you probably haven't conducted a backyard bird count before. It's a simple activity, but it can teach you and your friends quite a bit about birds, including how to recognize their calls and when and where to look. It's also a lot of fun, and you might be surprised at what you find. Best of all, you don't need any gear at all, though a field guide to birds, binoculars, and a smartphone camera are handy.

WHAT YOU'LL NEED

• A notepad and a pen or pencil, to record your finds

• A field guide, binoculars, and a smartphone camera (optional)

WHAT TO DO

To conduct your count, pick a 15-minute time slot for everyone to look for birds. Go to your backyard, or even a balcony, with a notepad and something to write with, and quietly look and listen for birds. Look near feeders, if you have them; see if you can spy birds flitting about in cover or perched in trees, and especially near garden areas. Even potted plants or container gardens sometimes have birds, like house finches, in them.

Wherever you are, but especially in the city or the suburbs, look for birds soaring overhead. A place where lots of people live might not seem like a birding hot spot, but because major cities are often near rivers and usually have plenty of pigeons and songbirds, they're often home to nesting groups of birds like peregrine falcons, which hunt the other birds for food.

When someone spots a bird, point it out—again, quietly—and try to snag a zoomed-in shot (it doesn't have to be perfect, just enough to help with identification). Then record what kind of birds they are, if you recognize them, how many birds you spotted, and what they were doing. If you don't recognize a bird and didn't get a picture of it, sketch out a quick drawing or make notes about its appearance, color, and size. Then you can check a field guide or photos online to try to identify it.

BIRD CALLS

You may hear a bird without seeing it—and this will happen more than you'd think. If you recognize the call, mark it down and add it to your count. If you don't know the call (again, this will happen pretty often), head online after your count to a website like All About Birds (www.allaboutbirds.org), and listen to recordings of birds that could help you figure it out.

RECORD YOUR FINDS

After you're done counting birds for 15 minutes, combine all of your finds into a list, and then consider setting up an account on a community science site such as eBird. There, you can create a "life list" of species spotted over time, and you'll also contribute to science—the resulting maps help create a snapshot of bird life over time.

DO A BACKYARD BIRD COUNT

THE CHRISTMAS BIRD COUNT

Once you get the hang of doing a bird count, consider participating in a national one. There are two long-running bird counts. One is The Christmas Bird Count, which has been around for 120 years. It takes place from mid-December to early January, and volunteers spread out to count birds in specific areas around each state and the country, with counts occurring in each local area for only one day. (So if you want to join in on the fun, tell your parents and prepare ahead of time!) To find out more, visit www.audubon.org/conservation/science/christmas-bird-count.

THE GREAT BACKYARD BIRD COUNT

This bird count is similar to the Christmas Bird Count, but it takes place everywhere, and you can participate if you spot birds for as little as 15 minutes, making it easy to join. It takes place in February. For more information and to sign up, visit gbbc.birdcount.org.

1. Keep track of the birds you see or spot here!

_____

_____

_____

_____

_____

_____

Backyard Bird Count   Feb. 2020
                      Peppermint Stick Plate

RED-TAiled Hawk × 1   Duration —
American Crow × 3   20 minutes
Black-capped chickadee × 1
Northern cardinal × 1

65

PLANT A HUMMINGBIRD, BEE & BUTTERFLY GARDEN

One way you can help wildlife wherever you live is by making your area a bit wilder. The easiest way to do that is to plant native plants. You don't need a huge amount of space to do this; even a small container garden with native plants can help attract—and feed—pollinators.

WHAT TO DO

Here are a few examples of how to attract some of the more sought-after pollinators:

• Common sunflowers are easy to grow (sometimes they grow themselves when birds drop seeds), and they attract bumblebees, flies, and colorful beetles.

• Planting milkweed (Common Milkweed, Butterfly Milkweed, Pink Swamp Milkweed, Showy Milkweed) attracts Monarch Butterflies. The females lay their eggs on the plant, and the caterpillars munch away on the milkweed and can be spotted if you take a close look.

• Plants with long tubular flowers, such as Wild Bergamot, attract hummingbirds and sphinx moths (large moths that are sometimes mistaken for hummingbirds).

Let the "weeds" be: dandelions, Common Blue Violets, and plants like White Clover provide bees, butterflies, and other beneficial insects with needed resources, and not only are these plants pretty and great to walk on (clover doesn't get crunchy like turfgrass does), they're tough and they don't need much care at all.

For a dedicated list, see this excellent write-up at the website for the Xerces Society: www.xerces.org/pollinator-conservation/pollinator-friendly-plant-lists.

A bumblebee on Buttonbush

1. Once you plant your hummingbird, bee, and butterfly
garden, keep track of the insects and birds you spot here!

_____

_____

_____

_____

_____

_____

SET UP A
WINDOW FEEDER

If you want to get an up-close look at birds, put up a window feeder. These transparent ledge-style feeders attach to a window via suction cups, and once the birds get used to the feeder and your presence on the other side of the glass, birds will chow down, enabling you to watch them from almost no distance at all.

BIRD NEST CAMS

For a different kind of up-close look at birds, head online and look at the many different nest cams offered on various bird sites. There are online nest cams for eagles hawks, ospreys, even hummingbirds.

For a list, visit www.allaboutbirds.org/cams.

MAKE YOUR WINDOWS SAFER FOR BIRDS

Hundreds of millions of birds are killed or injured each year when they accidentally fly into windows, often because they saw a reflection of nearby plants or the sky and thought it was a safe place to fly. Such collisions are often deadly, and they are a constant problem.

WHAT TO DO

There are a few simple safety steps you can take to help:

1. Close your blinds or curtains—this will make the window look more like a barrier. This is very important at night, when a lit-up room might seem like a welcoming place for a bird to fly.

2. When placing bird feeders, either keep them far away from windows (more than 20 feet) or keep them very close to windows—either directly on the window, using suction cups, or just a few feet away. (Even if a bird flies into a window from a close-by feeder, it won't fly fast enough to get seriously hurt.)

3. "Scare tape" or "flash tape"—reflective ribbons in iridescent colors that birds don't like—can be effective in keeping birds away from your windows.

4. Placing ribbons, pinwheels, and other moving accessories in front of windows can also scare birds away.

5. Keep plants away from windows, as birds often mistake them for part of the natural scenery outdoors.

WILDLIFE REHABILITATION NEAR YOU

If you see an animal get hurt or find one that you know is injured, keep your pets indoors and then contact your local wildlife rehabilitation center or a permit-carrying wildlife rehabilitation expert. To find one, check the website for your state's department of natural resources or department of fish and wildlife.

WHAT TO DO

If you find what you think is an orphaned baby animal and it's in a safe spot, don't pick it up. Instead, call your local wildlife rehabilitation center first—the animal might not actually be orphaned at all (its parents may be nearby or gathering food), and handling or disturbing the animal might actually harm it. When in doubt, just leave the animal alone and call an expert.

Note: North Dakota currently doesn't grant permits to new wildlife rehabilitators, but the rest of the states in the Midwest do.

This Dark-Eyed Junco was trapped in our garage and released unharmed.

1. Have you ever encountered an injured animal? What happened to it? Were you able to help it? Write your story here.

_____

_____

_____

_____

_____

_____

_____

_____

_____

_____

_____

_____

_____

_____

_____

ASSEMBLING A COLLECTION OF STATE MINERALS & GEMS

As with state birds or state flowers, most states in the Midwest have state gems or minerals, but you may not have heard or know about all of them. Still, state rocks and minerals are almost always selected for their long history in the state and economic impact or for their beauty, or both. Better yet, many of these state gems, minerals, and fossils are easy to collect!

Note: State symbols are approved by each state's legislature (the elected officials who make laws), so not every state has approved the same categories. That's why some states have more than others. What's more, some state fossils, (like the *Triceratops* in South Dakota) are not legal to collect, so I've left those out below.

Important Note: Before you go out collecting, make sure that collecting is allowed where you're looking for rocks. Don't go onto private property when collecting, because that's against the law. In many cases, there are public places where you can legally collect rocks, though it might take some homework first!

QUICK DEFINITION

A **mineral** usually consists of a combination of chemical elements. For example, table salt is a mineral (also known as halite) made of two elements, sodium and chlorine. Sometimes, a single **chemical element** (like gold or silver) can be found in nature; those are considered minerals too. A **rock** is a combination of at least two minerals.

ILLINOIS

FLUORITE

Often found in vibrant colors, fluorite is a mineral made up of two elements: fluorine and calcium. Fluorite gets its name because it is often fluorescent (that is, it glows under ultraviolet light). For decades, Illinois mines were one of the main producers of fluorite, but today those mines are closed, and finding specimens requires a lot of homework. Small pieces are often sold online, though fancier ones get very expensive.

INDIANA

SALEM LIMESTONE

Indiana's limestone is famous, adorning all sorts of famous buildings, from the Empire State Building in New York City to the Pentagon near Washington, D.C. Limestone is a sedimentary rock that formed as ancient organisms died and then settled into layers at the bottom of huge, shallow seas that covered the earth millions of years ago; this process is called **sedimentation.** Today, Salem Limestone—which comes from a large limestone deposit in south-central Indiana called the Salem Formation—remains a popular material, and it is sold widely.

IOWA

GEODE

Geodes can form in different ways, but the end result is the same: a geode is a round rock with an often boring-looking exterior, but its hollow interior is lined with crystals. The fun of geodes is both finding them and then breaking them open (carefully), because you never know what you're going to get. The city of Keokuk, Iowa, is famous for the many beautiful geodes found there and the wide variety of minerals hiding inside them. Better yet, there are many tour groups and businesses that allow visitors to hunt for geodes!

ASSEMBLING A COLLECTION OF STATE MINERALS & GEMS

KANSAS

GREENHORN LIMESTONE

Like Indiana, Kansas has limestone as its official state rock. Greenhorn Limestone is found in the central part of the state, in what used to be a seabed. The limestone contains a variety of fossils, from the remains of tiny algae to ammonites and other sea creatures. Kansas limestone has long been used as a construction material as well, even in fenceposts as shown here.

GALENA

Like much of the Midwest, Kansas has a long history of lead and zinc mining, producing huge amounts of the metals between World War I and World War II. Today those mines have closed, but Galena from Kansas is still sold in some rock shops.

Safety Note: Galena is pretty safe to handle occasionally, but avoid dusty specimens of it, and always wash your hands well after handling it.

JELINITE

Jelinite is an incredibly rare type of fossil amber that formed in the Cretaceous Period (145 million–66 million years ago), when dinosaurs and other prehistoric animals roamed the earth. This amber is gorgeous, and was discovered in only one location: in Ellsworth County. Specimens that survive today go for very high prices, and the reason is simple: the original area where jelinite was found has since been submerged under a massive lake!

Note: Jelinite looks even cooler than the amber shown in this photo; it has beautiful banding, but it's incredibly hard to find today!

MICHIGAN

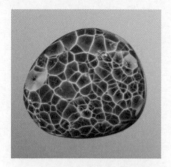

ISLE ROYALE GREENSTONE

Also known as Chlorastrolite, Isle Royale Greenstone is almost exclusively found on Isle Royale, a national park where collecting is forbidden. Famous for its greenish-white color and unique "turtle shell" pattern, it can be collected only on the Keweenaw Peninsula, where small pieces are sometimes found.

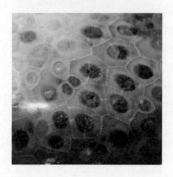

PETOSKEY STONE

Petoskey Stones are actually fossils of a specific kind of coral: *Hexagonaria percarinata*. The coral gets its genus name (*Hexagonaria*) because it has six sides. When found on the beach, these stones are often dull and hard to identify, but when polished, they are beautiful and show just how close together these corals lived. Hunting for Petoskey Stones is allowed at many public beaches, but you should always check first to make sure it's OK before you go collecting. Petoskey and Charlevoix are two of the best hunting locations, and many rock shops have them as well!

MINNESOTA

LAKE SUPERIOR AGATE

A unique variety of chalcedony (a type of quartz with very small crystals), Lake Superior Agates are famous for their colorful bands of often-bright colors, especially in reds, whites, and oranges. As their name suggests, Lake Superior Agates are easiest to find near the North Shore of Lake Superior in Minnesota, but thanks to the glaciers of the most recent ice age, they can be found across a good portion of the Midwest, including in rocky farm fields, in landscaping rocks, along dirt roads, and anywhere else Lake Superior gravel and rocks are used. If you're interested in hunting for these gorgeous stones, check out the many field guides about them (see page 132), or join an agates group online!

ASSEMBLING A COLLECTION OF STATE MINERALS & GEMS

MISSOURI

GALENA

Like Wisconsin, Missouri has selected Galena, mined as the primary source of the metal lead, as its state mineral. Missouri was home to several lead districts. Many lead mines have long since closed, but mining is active today in southeastern Missouri (also known as the Lead Belt). Samples of Missouri lead are available for sale in rock shops and online.

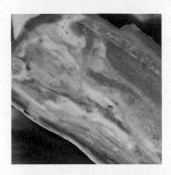

MOZARKITE

The name of this gorgeous variety of chert is a combination of the abbreviation for Missouri (*Mo*), and a nod to the Ozarks (*zark*). It's found mostly in west-central Missouri. Pieces of it can be purchased online and in rock shops, and you can find your own if you get help from a local rock-and-mineral club.

CRINOID

Known as sea lilies, these ancient animals have existed for more than 300 million years. Well-preserved fossils in limestone resemble something like an underwater flower, but these animals are actually filter feeders that are related to animals such as starfish. Crinoid "stems" consisted of many little O-shaped circles; these hard "Cheerios" are among the most common remains of crinoids found. Because a good portion of Missouri was once covered by a shallow sea, limestone (and the animals preserved in it) is quite common.

Note: This photo shows a crinoid fossil similar to those found in Missouri.

NEBRASKA

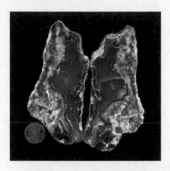

BLUE CHALCEDONY

A unique type of chalcedony (the same material found in agates), this beautiful blue form is popular with collectors and is used to make jewelry. It's found in the northwestern part of the state.

PRAIRIE AGATE

Like other agates, prairie agates are a banded form of chalcedony, though prairie agates tend to be a little duller in color and have less-defined bands than other agates. But some are absolutely gorgeous, and they are pretty common and easy to find. One place to look is Oglala National Grassland, where rock collecting is permitted, but, as always, check first to make sure it isn't against the rules in a specific spot.

NORTH DAKOTA

TEREDO PETRIFIED WOOD

When trees die, sometimes they get covered up with mud or other material, and over time, if the trees don't break down, mineral-rich water can seep in—this turns the wood into stone. In scientific terms, the wood is said to **petrify,** or **fossilize.** Petrified wood is cool enough by itself, because even after it fossilizes, it still looks like wood: it keeps the original shape and form of the wood's grains, bark, even things like holes in the tree. Well, Teredo (ter-ee-doe) Petrified Wood is even cooler. It started with wood being attacked by worm-like Teredo Clams. Then some of this wood petrified, dramatic holes and all, making for some amazing fossils. Finding Teredo Petrified Wood will likely be hard on your own, but similar specimens can be found at online shops.

Note: Teredo Petrified Wood is extremely hard to come by—this picture shows an example of similar petrified wood from Australia.

ASSEMBLING A COLLECTION OF STATE MINERALS & GEMS

OHIO

STATE FOSSIL: TRILOBITE (*ISOTELUS*)

Like Wisconsin (see the next page), Ohio has a trilobite as its state fossil. Ohio's trilobites date back more than 400 million years, and you can find traces of them in southwestern Ohio, in limestone near Cincinnati. Whole specimens are rare, mainly because individuals of this genus reached up to 15 inches long, and maybe even larger.

STATE GEMSTONE: OHIO FLINT

Flint is a form of chert, a sedimentary rock that formed when ancient sea life died and broke down. Chert and flint aren't usually all that exciting as rocks go, but Ohio's flint is different: it's brightly colored, it's famous for being used to create jewelry, and it has long been used by Indigenous peoples to make tools, knives, and so on. Found in the aptly named Flint Ridge, east of Columbus, Flint Ridge State Memorial has a museum and ancient flint pits, and there are pay-to-dig sites in the area.

SOUTH DAKOTA

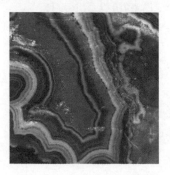

FAIRBURN AGATE

Like Lake Superior Agates (see page 75), Fairburn Agates are a form of banded chalcedony, but they formed in sedimentary rocks (limestone) instead of in igneous rocks. These agates are easy to identify because of their vibrant colors and because their banding has sharper angles (sometimes even looking leaf-like) than those in other agates. Fairburn Agates are named for Fairburn, South Dakota, and finding them takes some real effort. But rock shops in the area often have them on display, though even small samples can be quite expensive.

ROSE QUARTZ

Rose Quartz is the name for the pink form of quartz. Quartz is a very common mineral, and in much of South Dakota, Rose Quartz gets its pink color from a special mineral called dumortierite. Rose Quartz is found in western South Dakota; if you want to try to find your own, collecting is allowed at the Buffalo Gap National Grassland, though you'll definitely need an adult's help, be mindful of weather and critters, and so on.

WISCONSIN

STATE MINERAL: GALENA

Once widespread throughout the state, Galena is a mineral made of lead and sulfur. It was incredibly important in Wisconsin's history, as it was found in much of the southwestern portion of the state. Lead mining soon became a major part of the economy in Wisconsin, and the resulting lead was used in bullets, pipes, and, before the bad health effects of lead poisoning were known, even in the tubes that held toothpaste! Today, Galena is harder to find than it once was, but if you look (or ask an experienced expert) you can find it. Rock shops also have fine specimens for sale.

STATE FOSSIL: TRILOBITE (*CALYMENA CELEBRA*)

Trilobites are crustacean-like animals that lived in ancient seas that once covered much of the Midwest, including Wisconsin. Extinct today, their fossils still remain, some 400 million years later, but Wisconsin's state trilobite isn't that easy to find today.

QUICK QUIZ

1. Which of the above materials are fossils?

_____

_____

Answer on page 136!

TESTING THE HARDNESS OF MINERALS

Hardness is a useful way to help identify your mineral finds. The **Mohs Hardness Scale**, on the right, ranks some common minerals in terms of hardness, or how easily they can be scratched. Talc, the lowest mineral on the scale, is so soft you can scratch it with your fingers. Diamond is famous for being one of the hardest minerals, and for good reason: almost no natural substances can scratch it.

Making your own hardness test kit is a good way to start learning hands-on with rocks and minerals. Determining a mineral's hardness is a good first step in trying to identify it.

The way the scale works is simple: any material lower on the scale can be scratched by materials above it. So gypsum can scratch talc, but talc can't scratch gypsum. Similarly, calcite, which is a 3, can scratch gypsum *and* talc.

WHAT YOU'LL NEED

Using the scale to test your finds usually goes like this: You find a mineral (not a rock!) and you're not sure what it is. You start out by trying to scratch it with your fingernail. If it leaves a scratch, then it's softer than 2.5 on the scale. Chances are, however, it won't leave a scratch. So you need to move up to a different piece of equipment with a known hardness.

Here are some common, easy-to-find examples:

• Fingernail: 2.5

• A real piece of copper (not a penny, as these coins aren't made of much copper anymore): 3

• Steel nail or a knife: 5.5–6 (for safety reasons, you should have an adult help you with these tests)

• A piece of quartz: 7

Talc
$Mg_3Si_4O_{10}(OH)_2$

Gypsum
$CaSO_4 \cdot 2H_2O$

Calcite
$CaCO_3$

Fluorite
CaF_2

Apatite
$Ca_5(PO_4)_3(F,Cl,OH)$

WHAT TO DO

To scratch it, you need to hold the to-be-scratched mineral firmly in one hand, and use a pointed area of the "scratching" mineral and press firmly, away from your body or fingers. If it leaves a scratch mark, it's softer than the "scratching" mineral. Obviously, for safety reasons you should make sure you have an adult conduct the actual scratch tests—don't handle a knife or a nail yourself.

Once you've found something that scratches it, you're pretty close to figuring out its hardness. Then it's often a matter of scratching it with other minerals from the chart or your scratching tools, then seeing if you can figure out an even more specific range. Once you've narrowed down the hardness some more, looking up mineral hardness is easy online.

Note: You can also buy lab-calibrated "hardness pick" kits; these are much more accurate, but they can be expensive.

1. Keep track of your hardness tests here. Doing so can help you learn to identify your finds!

_____

_____

_____

_____

_____

_____

_____

_____

Orthoclase
$KAlSi_3O_8$

Quartz
SiO_2

Topaz
$Al_2SiO_4(F,OH)_2$

Corundum
Al_2O_3

Diamond
C

LOOKING AT SOIL, DIRT, OR A DEAD LOG

Rocks and minerals are definitely showier than plain old dirt or soil, but that's only until you get an up-close look. Once you do, with a magnifying glass, a macro camera, or a small microscope, you'll be surprised at what you find.

WHAT TO DO

Roll over a dead log and strip off a piece of bark. A dead log might look, well, dead, but it's actually its own little world. Insects, such as wasps, burrow into the wood to lay their eggs. Under the bark, ants and beetles are busy tunneling or making a home (they often leave behind intricate patterns on the wood). And it's easy to spot tiny mushrooms and sometimes very colorful slime molds, which are often food sources for other animals, such as slugs, snails, and insects. Once you start looking closely, it's easy to find a lot more life forms than you might expect.

Important Note: If you have venomous spiders or snakes in your area, make sure you go out with an adult and take proper precautions (wear gloves, long pants, and so on) when digging in dirt or turning over logs.

WHAT YOU MIGHT SEE

- Slugs or tiny land snails
- Lichen (an organism that consists of algae and/or bacteria and fungi, all living together)
- Slime molds
- Spiders, ants, tiny insects, and other animals

QUICK QUESTIONS

1. How many types of life did you find?

_____

_____

2. Were you able to identify them all?

_____

_____

MAKE A CAST OF AN ANIMAL TRACK

You might think that animal tracks won't last very long, but that's not always true. You can actually preserve a track using plaster. Follow the instructions below to make your very own track cast!

WHAT YOU'LL NEED

- A strip of plastic or cardboard long enough to wrap around your track
- A paper clip
- Plaster of Paris
- A container for mixing

WHAT TO DO

1. Remove any twigs or leaves around the track.

2. Use the plastic or cardboard to create a "wall" around the track. Use the paper clip to secure the ends together.

3. Add two parts dry plaster for every one part water (so if you use 1 cup of dry plaster, you should use $1/2$ cup of water).

4. Mix the plaster and water together until it's like pancake batter. Stir until the plaster isn't lumpy, usually at least a few minutes.

5. Pour the plaster inside your wall (but not directly onto the track), letting the plaster flow over the track gradually. Pour enough to cover the entire track to a depth of about $3/4$ inch.

6. Wait half an hour, then test the firmness of the plaster. Once it's hard enough, remove it by grabbing it at the edges. Wait a few days for it to dry completely, and you then can frame it or put it on display.

Have an adult help you when creating a cast, as it can be a bit tricky. Once you have a cast, you can even frame it.

MAKE A SELF-PORTRAIT USING NATURE

WHAT YOU WILL NEED

• Several blank pieces of paper

• A glue stick, if you want to create a permanent piece of art

WHAT TO DO

With an adult, start out by gathering some twigs; these are great for creating a general outline of your face. Then start thinking about the color of your skin, hair, and eyes, and look around for natural objects that are a close match. It's best to choose from things that you know are safe to touch: rocks and pebbles, sand, dandelions, flower petals, oaks, maples, grass, moss, tree bark, and so on. If you're not sure if you can touch it, leave it be, or ask an adult. That way, you can avoid poison ivy, poison oak, poison sumac, and anything icky.

When you're done, take a picture of your portrait, and throw any leftovers away. If you want to keep it, you can glue each object to the paper and then frame it. Just make sure no little kids have access to the actual leaves and flowers and such.

GEOLOGY & GEMSTONES CROSSWORD

ACROSS

1. Often found in beautiful reds and whites, Minnesota's state gem is easiest to find near Lake Superior, but it can also be found across several states in the Midwest.

5. Several states have this animal as their state fossil; extinct today, they looked like weird bugs, and they lived in ancient oceans.

6. This beautiful gemstone is found in South Dakota, but it can be very hard to find.

8. This hard form of quartz is Ohio's state mineral, which is very colorful.

10. If you like pink, look for this state mineral of South Dakota, where lots of it can be found.

11. This sedimentary rock formed when ancient marine creatures died and their skeletons sank to the bottom of the sea; this rock often contains fossils and is popular as a building material because of its yellow-tan color and its hardness.

DOWN

2. From the outside, these rocks don't look that exciting, but when you break them open, you'll find neat crystals inside.

3. The world's major source of the metal lead, this mineral was mined in many states of the Midwest.

4. If the conditions are just right, tree parts and wood can be replaced by minerals, creating this material.

7. During the last ice age, which ended about 10,000 years ago, these rivers of ice scoured the landscape.

9. Also known as sea lilies, these animals lived in ancient oceans; today, they're very common fossils across the Midwest, though most fossils are simply Cheerio-shaped stem fragments.

Answers on page 137!

One of the best places to hunt for rocks is along Lake Superior!

LEARNING TO IDENTIFY BASIC GROUPS OF BUGS

If you want to learn about insects, start by learning to identify the basic groups (or orders) of insects. Some, such as butterflies and moths, you might already know, but there are quite a few more to discover. This list isn't all-inclusive, but it gives you a fun idea of some of the insects you can find!

ANTS, BEES & WASPS *(HYMENOPTERA)*

Honeybee

Bumblebee

Metallic Green Sweat Bee

Tricolored Bee

Carpenter Ant

Yellowjacket

Giant Ichneumon Wasp

Pigeon Tremex Horntail

BUTTERFLIES & MOTHS (*LEPIDOPTERA*)

White-Lined Sphinx Moth

Io Moth

Celery Looper

Chickweed Geometer

Monarch Butterfly

Viceroy Butterfly

Eastern Tiger Swallowtail

Fiery Skipper

FLIES (*DIPTERA*)

Hover Fly

House Fly

Long-Legged Fly

Margined Calligrapher Fly

LEARNING TO IDENTIFY
BASIC GROUPS OF BUGS

BEETLES (*COLEOPTERA*)

Cucumber Beetle

Six-Spotted Tiger Beetle

Potato Beetle

Goldenrod Soldier Beetle

Thistle Tortoise Beetle

Japanese Beetle (invasive)

Stag Beetle

Red Milkweed Beetle

MISCELLANEOUS

Mayflies
Ephemeroptera

Lacewing
Neuroptera

Grasshopper
Orthoptera

Walking Stick
Phasmatodea

TRUE BUGS (*HEMIPTERA*)

Pale Green
Assassin Bug

Cicada

Leafhopper

Milkweed Bugs

Treehopper

Western Conifer
Seed Bug

North American
Tarnished Plant
Bug

Stinkbug

DAMSELFLIES & DRAGONFLIES (*ODONATA*)

Ebony Jewelwing
Damselfy

Four-Spotted
Skimmer
Dragonfly

Meadowhawk
Dragonfly

Damselfly
(close-up)

LEARNING TO IDENTIFY BASIC GROUPS OF BUGS

NON-INSECTS

Centipede

Millipede

Isopod

Worm

Bronze Jumping Spider

Cobweb Spider

Wolf Spider

Orb-Weaver Spider

1. In which month do you see the most insects where you live?

_____

_____

_____

_____

_____

MAKE YOUR YARD
A LITTLE WILDER

Many insect populations are at risk. Habitat destruction, insecticide spraying (which kills a lot more than just mosquitoes), and water pollution can all play a role. Lawns, in particular, are part of the problem, as they are incredibly widespread, and not all that useful for many plants and animals. That's why it's helpful to make your yard a bit wilder.

WHAT TO DO

With your parents' OK, make a portion of your yard a little bit more like nature. Plant a mix of native flowering plants there, don't spray pesticides or herbicides in that area or mow it as heavily, and leave out some deadwood for insect habitat. Then, over time, keep track of the critters you find, and compare it to the rest of your yard. You'll find that even a small patch of plants can attract critters you may have never seen before.

1. Before you create a "wild patch" in your yard, write down your plan below. What are you hoping to attract?

_____

_____

_____

_____

RAISE NATIVE CATERPILLARS & RELEASE THEM

Finding a caterpillar is one of the highlights of spring and summer. But unless it's a really well-known caterpillar, like a Monarch, identifying caterpillars can be tricky for beginners. Many caterpillars, including all of the classic inchworms, will actually end up being moths. Even the name scientists use for these moths—Geometridae—is a reference to geometry and how these caterpillars "measure" as they walk.

But you don't need to identify your caterpillar to rear it; after all, one of the most fun ways to identify a moth or a butterfly is after it's turned into an adult!

WHAT YOU'LL NEED

• A butterfly house (it's best to purchase a high-quality one online first)

• An ample supply of fresh leaves

• A water source for the leaves, but one that the caterpillar can't enter (pill bottles work great)

WHAT TO DO

When you find a caterpillar, immediately note what plant you find it on or, if it's on the ground, the plants that are nearby. These are likely the caterpillar's host plants (the ones it needs to eat to become an adult). If you're unsure of which plants to gather, bring in a sampling of several different kinds. If you want an exact answer, post a photo of your caterpillar on a site like BugGuide.net and ask for help on finding out what it eats.

Once you have the caterpillar and the host plants, you'll need to ready your butterfly house. Many common commercially available houses are mesh cylinders.

First, you need to prepare your water source for the host plants. Do not provide a water dish or another water source at the bottom of a butterfly house; caterpillars drown easily. Instead, have a parent help you drill or cut a hole in a small container like an old pill bottle, and put the plant stems into the water source (but make sure the caterpillar can't fall into the water and drown).

Over time, you'll need to replace the leaves, and clean up its poop (known as frass). Eventually, the caterpillar will begin to pupate. This is a fascinating process in its own right, but watching one emerge is even better.

Of course, things can go wrong when collecting wild caterpillars: parasitic wasps often attack or infest caterpillars; if your cage is dirty, they can get sick; and if you find a caterpillar in late summer, it might be one that overwinters as a pupa. Still, with practice, there's a good chance that you'll get to watch moths and butterflies all summer long if you work at it hard enough!

GET TO KNOW THE MIDWEST'S NATIVE BEES

If you've been following the news, you know that bee populations are in trouble. But you're probably most familiar with honeybees, which are actually an introduced species native to Europe, not the U.S. Think of honeybees as farm animals. Those honeybees you see in your yard? In a sense, those are kind of like escaped chickens or cows.

Domesticated honeybee populations have run into trouble over the past few decades due to a combination of factors, including pests (especially the Varroa mite), pesticide use, and habitat loss. These domesticated insects play a critical role in pollinating agricultural crops, especially almonds, blueberries, and cherries.

Honeybees aren't the only bees in the U.S. that are threatened; on the contrary, while honeybees get much of the press, there are thousands of native bee species in the

QUICK QUIZ

Which one of these is a bee?

1.

2.

3.

Answers on page 136!

U.S., and many of them are threatened or endangered due to habitat loss, loss of suitable nesting sites, and the like. They range from the familiar bumblebees that flutter along your flowers to carpenter bees, which bore into wood.

BEES

Bumblebee

Carpenter Bee

Mining Bee

Mason Bee

Sweat Bee

BEE LOOK-ALIKES & BEETLES

Flower Fly

Ornate Snipe Fly

Locust Borer Beetle

START AN INSECT COLLECTION

If you love bugs, creating a bug collection can help you observe them up close, but if you're not into killing bugs, there's another option. When you're out in nature, chances are you'll notice dead insects if you're paying attention. If a bug is dead but in reasonably good shape, you can add it to your collection. You'll be surprised at what you find: butterflies and moths, gorgeous beetles, and so on (after all, insects don't live very long).

One of the easiest ways to store insects is with a Riker Mount, a simple glass case with padding that holds the insects against the glass.

OPTIONAL PROJECT

If you want to collect live samples, placing them in a zip-top plastic bag and freezing them is one way to kill them humanely. On sites like BugGuide.net, you can also look up "killing jars" online that use common household chemicals.

1. What is your favorite type of insect? Why?

_____

_____

_____

_____

_____

_____

MAKE AN ULTRAVIOLET BUG TRAP

Have you ever noticed how bugs are attracted to lights at night? This happens because nocturnal insects use light to navigate, and artificial lights confuse them. With a simple setup, you can set up your own "light trap" to attract bugs. It's a wonderful way to see insects you might not otherwise see.

WHAT YOU'LL NEED

- A lantern, an ultraviolet lamp. or a blacklight (available online)

- An extension cord

- An old bedsheet or a curtain (a light-colored one is best)

- Two sections of rope

- A pair of scissors

- Flashlights

- A camera

WHAT TO DO

With an adult supervising, cut holes in the corners at one end of the bedsheet, and have the adult help you tie a section of rope to each hole in the bedsheet or curtain. (Curtains often have ready-made loops that make things easier.)

Then look for a good spot to find bugs; generally, the wilder it is, the better, but you'll need to be within reach of an outdoor-safe extension cord so you can plug in your light. Near woods, bushes, or other plants is good, but even the middle of a suburban yard will have all sorts of bugs you've likely never seen.

Tie one rope to a tree branch, a bird feeder hook, or another support, then pull the rope on the other side of the curtain until the whole thing is taut, hanging like a movie screen. Tie that rope to a chair or anything else heavy enough to hold it. About an hour before sundown, find a chair and place it on either side of the curtain, set your light on it, and plug the into the extension cord, shining it onto the curtain (but not close enough to touch it).

Then wait and make periodic visits to the sheet to see what you find! Heading out with a flashlight in one hand and a camera in another is an easy way to record your finds (and identify them later on).

Once you get a look at the insects you've attracted, wait a while longer and visit again later in the night (some of the best bug hunting is late at night).

Note: When you are observing moths, the light might shine on you and your clothes a bit, so it's possible (though not all that likely) to have moths or other bugs land on you. To avoid this, wear a dark shirt (not one that matches the "moth sheet"). A few bugs may land on you, but gently brushing them off with a stick or a gloved hand is enough to make them fly away.

CRICKET MATH

Crickets are famously noisy insects; the males rub their front wings (not their legs!) together to attract females. That much, you probably knew. But did you know that you can count a cricket's chirps to tell the approximate temperature outside?

The math is simple: Go outside and listen for a cricket that's chirping. Count the number of its chirps for 13 seconds, then add 40 to that total. Then check it against the temperature for your area: go to www.noaa.gov and find your local weather in the top-right corner.

Pretty wild, right? Try it again on a different day and record your findings below.

The reason this works out is actually relatively simple: Crickets, like all insects, are cold-blooded, so their body temperature depends on the surrounding air. So when it's warmer, their metabolism speeds up, and so do the chirps! When it's colder, their chirps slow down.

Number of chirps in 13 seconds _____ + 40 = _____

Number of chirps in 13 seconds _____ + 40 = _____

Number of chirps in 13 seconds _____ + 40 = _____

Number of chirps in 13 seconds _____ + 40 = _____

Number of chirps in 13 seconds _____ + 40 = _____

Number of chirps in 13 seconds _____ + 40 = _____

[1] Original research via Dr. Peggy LeMone and James Larsen. https://www.questia.com/library/journal/1G1-272666064/the-sound-of-crickets-using-evidence-based-reasoning

BUGS & INSECTS CROSSWORD

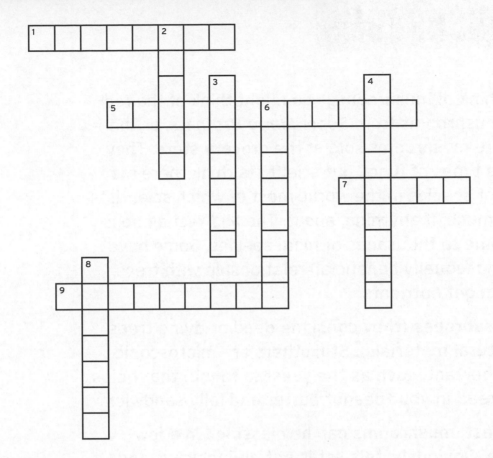

ACROSS

1. This insect is very important for many farmers, as it helps pollinate their crops, but it's not native to North America.

5. The word for the wiggly larvae (juveniles) of moths or butterflies.

7. Butterflies usually fly during the day; this group of related insects look similar, but most (but not all) fly at night.

9. This animal isn't an insect at all; robins love to eat them.

Answers on page 137!

DOWN

2. Fireflies are a type of this kind of insect.

3. This insect is famous for chirping at night, and by counting its chirps, you can even use it as a thermometer!

4. These beautiful, fast-flying insects zoom through the summer air, snatching bugs in midair.

6. This group of caterpillars is known to scientists as the geometers, but most people call them this, for how they seem to "measure out" distance as they walk along.

8. There are many different kinds of this red, spotted insect.

START LOOKING AT MUSHROOMS

When you think of mushrooms, you might think of the red-and-white mushrooms from *Super Mario Brothers*, or the familiar white mushrooms sold at the grocery store. They are only two types of fungi, but scientists think there may be millions of species in the world, most of which scientists don't know much, if anything, about. The Midwest alone is probably home to thousands of fungi species. Some have a **mutualistic** (equally beneficial) relationship with trees, helping them get nutrients.

Others are **saprobes** (they consume dead or dying trees or other natural materials). Still others are microscopic but very important, such as the yeast (a fungi!) that helps make the bread in your peanut butter and jelly sandwich.

In the Midwest, mushrooms can be classified in a few simple ways. Obviously, this list is not all-inclusive, and it won't replace a field guide (or five!), but these general categories are helpful to know.

Important Note: Do **not** eat wild mushrooms. Some are very **toxic** (poisonous) to eat and tricky to identify. Wait until you're older and have trained, experienced adults to help you out.

If you want to pick or touch a mushroom to get a closer look, wear gloves. And if you're making a spore print or a sketch, do that outside. Throw the mushrooms in the garbage when you're done.

CAP & STEM WITH GILLS

Mushrooms with a stem and a cap, with gills underneath.

Red Fly Agaric

Unidentified Find

Green-Spored Lepiota

Amethyst Laccaria

Yellow Fly Agaric

Marasmius

CAP & STEM WITH PORES

Mushrooms with a cap and a stem, but with tiny holes (pores) underneath.

Ash Bolete

Ash Bolete (underside)

Scaber Stalk

START LOOKING AT MUSHROOMS

SHELF MUSHROOMS

Mushrooms that mostly grow out from trees, like a shelf, or a bracket; they can have either pores or gills.

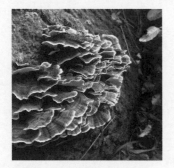   

Shelf Fungus
Artist's Conk
Chicken of the Woods
Chicken of the Woods (underside)

ROUND MUSHROOMS

Mushrooms that grow on the ground, in a ball or oval-like shape. Some puffballs can get as large as a soccer ball, and they're famous for "popping" and releasing a cloud of spores. But don't breathe in the dust—it can make you sick.

Puffball
Earthball
Earthstar

SURPRISING MUSHROOMS

Mushrooms that are hard to describe because of their brain-like shapes or weird consistency.

Dead Man's Fingers

Jelly Fungus

Wrinkled Peach

Coral Fungi

False Morel

Morel

TIPS FOR SPOTTING MUSHROOMS

- Look for mushrooms after a rain (they can pop up quite quickly).
- Look near the bases of dying trees or on dead logs.
- Mushrooms often seem to grow from the ground, but they might actually be growing from wood in the soil.
- Slime molds often grow under bark.

START LOOKING AT MUSHROOMS

SLIME MOLDS

Slime molds were once considered fungi, but they're now classified differently. Still, they are often grouped together with fungi, so here are a few! They're really weird, and by the way, they can move—but slowly, so you need a time-lapse camera to see it.

Dog Vomit Slime (gross!)

Chocolate Tube Slime Mold

Wolf's Milk Slime

1. Page through a field guide to mushrooms, then go and look for them in your area, especially if it has rained lately (mushrooms often spring up after rains). Jot down notes about them here! But remember: **Don't eat wild mushrooms.** Take notes and pictures instead!

_____

_____

_____

_____

_____

2. Sketch your mushroom finds here!

MAKE MUSHROOM SPORE PRINTS

Mushrooms reproduce via spores. Spores are too small to see individually without a microscope, but there's an easy and fun way to spot them: by making a spore print. For a number of technical reasons, spores aren't considered the same thing as a seed in a plant, but the basic idea is the same: spores help fungi reproduce. And they do that by leaving microscopic spores behind almost everywhere. Spore colors vary by species, and they can produce some neat results. To see for yourself, make a spore print.

WHAT YOU'LL NEED

• Small bowls or cups

• White paper and, if possible, some construction paper of various colors

• Different kinds of mushrooms, with caps and pores, or caps and gills

WHAT TO DO

With a knife, cut off the cap of each mushroom—or take a good section of a shelf mushroom—and place it on top of a piece of paper. (The gills or pores should be facing down onto the paper.) Place a small bowl or a cup over each mushroom. Mushroom spore colors vary a lot, so it's helpful to change up the paper color; a mushroom with light-colored spores won't show up well on white paper, for instance. Wait an hour or so, remove the bowl, and throw the mushroom in the trash. Then admire the spore print left behind!

Important Note: Have an adult handle the knife, and don't make spore prints in your kitchen or another area where food is served, or where someone could mistake the mushrooms for food. A garage is a good place to make spore prints.

CARVE ARTIST'S CONK

Artist's Conk is a special kind of shelf mushroom that grows on dead or dying trees. At first glance, it doesn't look like much. It's pretty plain looking on the top—oval shaped and brown and white—and underneath it's just a drab white.

Artist's Conk gets its name because its white pores turn a dark brown when scratched. And the scratches then stay that way, making it a favorite of "scratch artists." This makes Artist's Conk something like nature's Etch A Sketch.

Of course, to identify Artist's Conk, you'll need an adult's help and a field guide (see page 132), but it's not too tricky to spot once you start looking.

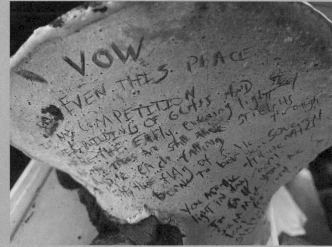

1. Before you carve your Artist's Conk, you might want to practice writing down your message here. When you're writing on a mushroom, you can't use an eraser, so practicing here first can help you get it right.

_____

_____

_____

_____

_____

_____

_____

_____

_____

_____

_____

_____

_____

SPOTTING THE MOON, THE PLANETS & ORION

In winter, it can be hard to stay active outside. After all, it's cold and it gets dark early, but for stargazers, winter is one of the best seasons around. There aren't any bugs, you don't have to stay up late for it to get really dark, and some of the best constellations are visible during the winter. So if you dress up warmly, grab a lawn chair, and bust out a small telescope or binoculars, you can see the planets, the moon, even the Orion Nebula and the Pleiades star cluster.

WHAT YOU WILL NEED

• Warm clothes

• A lawn chair

• A small telescope or, if you don't have one, binoculars

• A field guide and/or virtual planetarium software like Stellarium (which is free for Windows computers and Macs)

WHAT TO DO

First, figure out what you want to see before you head out. That's where a good field guide comes in. Virtual planetarium software is great too, because it can show you exactly what the sky will look like wherever you are (and whenever you want).

Starting with the moon is always a good idea, as it's bright and impossible to miss. The best time to observe the moon is in the "first quarter" when only one half of the moon is lit up, as it reveals a lot more detail than a full moon, when all that reflected sunlight washes out the view. If you have a small telescope, try holding a smartphone over the eyepiece, and see if you can snap some pictures. This can be tricky, but if you take a bunch of pictures and fiddle with the settings, you can get some wonderful shots (there are also phone mounts you can buy fairly inexpensively online, though you have to get the right model for your phone).

After you take a look at the moon, make sure you get a chance to see Jupiter, Saturn, Mars, and Venus. You'll need to refer to your field guide

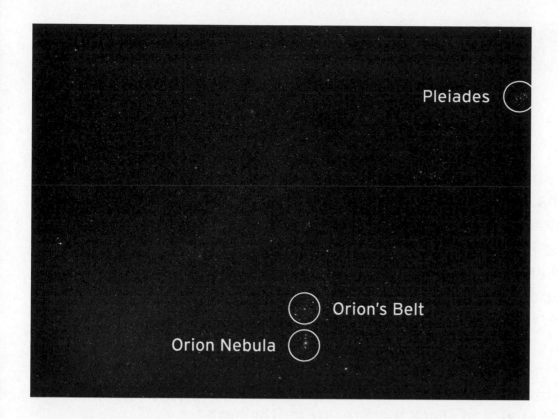

Pleiades

Orion's Belt

Orion Nebula

or planetarium software for when and where to look for each, because they appear to move through the sky over time. Still, it's worth the effort: seeing Saturn's rings for the first time will make you gasp.

Note: Don't expect to see the rings like you would in a picture from NASA—the planets will look pretty darn small. But if you're patient and you focus just right, you'll see the planets for real. It's an amazing experience. Even if you just have binoculars, you can often spot Jupiter's largest moons: Io, Europa, Ganymede, and Callisto.

Finally, even if you only have a small telescope or binoculars, make sure to take a look at the constellation Orion. Easy to spot throughout much of the late fall and winter, it's famous for Orion's Belt, a line of three evenly spaced stars at the center of the constellation. If you look just below the belt, you'll see a star that looks a bit smudged; it's actually not a star at all. It's a nebula, an area where stars are forming. Viewed through binoculars or a small telescope, it's a wonderful sight. The same is true for the Pleiades, a bright star cluster. To find it, simply follow from Orion's Belt up and to the right. If you're just looking with your eyes, it looks like a little smudge, but through binoculars or a telescope, it looks kind of like a miniature version of the Big Dipper.

View through binoculars

SPOT THE INTERNATIONAL SPACE STATION (ISS)

If you really want an amazing sight, see if you can observe the International Space Station as it passes overhead. Continuously inhabited by astronauts since the year 2000, the International Space Station is massive—longer than football field—and its huge solar panels reflect a lot of light back to Earth. This makes it incredibly bright in the night sky as it passes overhead.

WHAT TO DO

To spot it, visit the excellent website Spot the Station (spotthestation.nasa.gov), and check the forecast for the next times the station will pass overhead your location. It'll be visible either in the morning (sometimes quite early) or in the evening. But, if you are patient, there are quite a few options and you can make observing the ISS a fun habit (if you want a challenge, try snapping a photo of it as it passes overhead).

And once you spot it, you can visit the website www.howmany peopleareinspacerightnow.com to learn who was aboard the ISS as it flew by.

1. What was it like seeing the International Space Station?

_____

_____

2. How long did you see it, and how bright was it in the sky compared to the stars and planets?

_____

_____

 International
Space Station

CONDUCT A BACKYARD
BIO-BLITZ

A **bio-blitz** is an event where nature lovers—usually in a large group—try to record all of the life in a given area during a set period of time. But you don't need to be a scientist to do a bio-blitz; you can do one yourself or with your family. And you can do one wherever you are: in your backyard, on a trip, even from the window of a car or from an apartment balcony. The basic idea is simple: you want to try to identify as many life forms as you can within a certain amount of time.

WHAT YOU WILL NEED

• A magnifying glass

• A smartphone

• A notebook and pen for each person

• Field guides

WHAT TO DO

The simplest way to start off is in your backyard or a green space near where you live. Have an adult set a timer for 15 minutes. Start out with the easy stuff first: the grass, any weeds that you recognize (dandelions), and birds or mammals (such as chipmunks or squirrels). It's helpful to be systematic: start in one area, and look it over carefully before moving on to the next.

For each life form you find, write down what you think it is and where you found it. Take a picture, or draw it if you don't know what it is and want to look it up. See how many different kinds of animals and plants you can find and record them on the form to the right!

Bonus: If you can look it up, try to find the **scientific name** for what you found. Scientific names exist to make it easier for scientists to talk to each other clearly. For example, there are three main different kinds of bears in North America: Black Bears, Brown Bears, and Polar Bears. So the word *bear* isn't very specific. And for many creatures, including insects, there simply aren't any common names. A scientific name is a special name that has two parts: a **genus name,** which is like a last name and is shared with other similar animals, and a **species name**, which is like a first name. Together, that name is unique for that animal. For example, only one plant has the name *Taraxacum officinale*: the Common Dandelion, and scientists all over the world can refer to it, even if they don't speak the same language!

WHAT IS IT?	LOCATION	SCIENTIFIC NAME
Plants		
Dandelion	By the swing set	*Taraxacum officinale*
White Oak Tree	In the front yard	*Quercus alba*
Birds		
American Robin	On the oak tree	*Turdus migratorius*
Mammals		
Gray Squirrel	?	
Insects		
Unidentified but Cool		

CONTRIBUTE TO A COMMUNITY SCIENCE PROJECT

If your parents have a smartphone, or you have one of your own, ask if it's OK to download **iNaturalist.** This app is all about nature. It's a wonderful way to keep track of and identify your finds, and you can help science in the process.

WHAT TO DO

The way it works is simple. You sign up (you have to be 13 years old to have your own account), and then you take a photo of an animal, plant, or mushroom that you spot. You then create an observation, add the photo, and click on the "What Did You See?" button. The app will run the photo through a computer program that will attempt to identify it; the program isn't perfect, but it often helps you narrow down what you found.

Then, if you share the observation and location online, other observers (including experts) can help confirm your identification (or propose a new one). Once an observation has two identifications that are the same, it's considered "research grade" and it can be used by scientists!

In fact, this might happen faster than you think. I've had several scientists contact me about my photos, either because the species hadn't been recorded in that area or because they wanted a sample of the species. In short, it's an easy way to do a little real science yourself.

Note: If you or your parents are concerned about your privacy (ask them if you're not sure), you don't have to post your exact location—there's an option to click "Obscured" under "Geolocation." This will keep people from seeing exactly where you made your observation and instead only gives a large range instead.

1. Keep track of your community science discoveries here by making a "life list" of the plants, animals, and fungi you've spotted.

_____

_____

_____

_____

_____

_____

_____

_____

_____

_____

_____

_____

_____

NATURE BINGO

Circle the nature you see, and see who gets a bingo first!

NATURE

BINGO

MOSS	BEE	MAMMAL	WORM	DECIDUOUS TREE
ANT	BIRD	DANDELION	CONIFEROUS TREE	SPIDER
ROCK	LADYBUG	FREE SPACE THE SKY	PINE CONE	BEETLE
THE MOON	OAK LEAF	GRASS	STAR	FROG
MAPLE LEAF	LOG	MUSHROOM	CLOUD	BUTTERFLY

NATURE

B I N G O

DANDELION	BEE	MAMMAL	OAK LEAF	GRASS
CONIFEROUS TREE	ROCK	MOSS	LADYBUG	CLOUD
SPIDER	ANT	FREE THE SKY SPACE	BEETLE	DECIDUOUS TREE
THE MOON	WORM	BIRD	LOG	STAR
MUSHROOM	MAPLE LEAF	PINE CONE	BUTTERFLY	FROG

RECORD YOUR ACTIVITIES, DISCOVERIES & FINDS HERE

If you find something neat, make a sketch to the right to help you remember details so you can compare your drawing to a field guide or another reference later.

_____

_____

_____

_____

_____

_____

_____

_____

_____

_____

_____

_____

_____

RECORD YOUR ACTIVITIES, DISCOVERIES & FINDS HERE

If you find something neat, make a sketch to the right to help you remember details so you can compare your drawing to a field guide or another reference later.

_____

_____

_____

_____

_____

_____

_____

_____

_____

_____

_____

_____

RECORD YOUR ACTIVITIES, DISCOVERIES & FINDS HERE

If you find something neat, make a sketch to the right to help you remember details so you can compare your drawing to a field guide or another reference later.

_____

_____

_____

_____

_____

_____

_____

_____

_____

_____

_____

_____

RECORD YOUR ACTIVITIES, DISCOVERIES & FINDS HERE

If you find something neat, make a sketch to the right to help you remember details so you can compare your drawing to a field guide or another reference later.

_____

_____

_____

_____

_____

_____

_____

_____

_____

_____

_____

_____

RECOMMENDED READING

Daniels, Jaret C. *Backyard Bugs: An Identification Guide to Common Insects, Spiders, and More.* Cambridge, Minnesota: Adventure Publications, 2017.

Eisner, Thomas. *For Love of Insects.* Cambridge, Massachusetts: Belknap Press of Harvard University Press, 2003.

Himmelman, John. *Discovering Moths: Nighttime Jewels in Your Own Backyard.* Camden, Maine: Down East Books, 2002.

Lynch, Bob, and Dan R. Lynch. *Lake Superior Rocks & Minerals: A Field Guide to the Lake Superior Area.* Cambridge, Minnesota: Adventure Publications, 2008.

Lynch, Dan R. *Fossils for Kids: An Introduction to Paleontology.* Cambridge, Minnesota: Adventure Publications, 2020.

Lynch, Dan R. *Rock Collecting for Kids: An Introduction to Geology.* Cambridge, Minnesota: Adventure Publications, 2018.

Lynch, Dan R., and Bob Lynch. *Minnesota Rocks & Minerals: A Field Guide to the Land of 10,000 Lakes.* Cambridge, Minnesota: Adventure Publications, 2011.

Marrone, Teresa, and Kathy Yerich. *Mushrooms of the Upper Midwest.* Cambridge, Minnesota: Adventure Publications, 2020.

Poppele, Jonathan. *Night Sky: A Field Guide to the Constellations.* Cambridge, Minnesota: Adventure Publications, 2009.

Tekiela, Stan. *The Kids' Guide to Birds of Michigan: Fun Facts, Activities, and 86 Cool Birds.* Cambridge, Minnesota: Adventure Publications, 2018.

Tekiela, Stan. *The Kids' Guide to Birds of Minnesota: Fun Facts, Activities, and 85 Cool Birds.* Cambridge, Minnesota: Adventure Publications, 2018.

GLOSSARY

Amber Fossilized tree resin that is a popular gemstone; it also can contain insects or other signs of life preserved within it.

Biome A community of animals and plants that live in a specific kind of climate and environment.

Chalcedony A banded form of quartz that is popular as a collectible.

Chemical Element One of the 92 naturally occurring chemicals such as oxygen, carbon, etc., that make up all matter on Earth.

Commodities Farm products such as corn and soybeans that are sold worldwide.

Conifer A tree that produces seeds by cones. Most conifers, but not all, are evergreen (see below).

Evergreen A tree that doesn't lose its leaves but instead stays green all winter.

Extirpated Another word for animals being wiped out from their original habitat.

Fluorescent Glowing or giving off light after absorbing energy (especially ultraviolet light).

Galena A mineral that contains lead and sulfur. Galena is the primary source of the metal lead.

Game Bird A bird that is hunted for sport or for its meat.

Geode A round rock with an empty space inside that is often filled with crystals; when broken in half, geodes are popular collectibles.

Genus Name See **Scientific Name**.

Glaciers Huge rivers of ice that once covered much of the Midwest, creating a lot of the topography (landscapes) we see (or don't see) today.

GLOSSARY

Ice Age One of many periods in Earth's history of prolonged cold and glacial activity; the last ice age ended around 10,000 years ago.

Introduced Brought to an area instead of occurring naturally there (example: cows in the U.S.).

Invasive An introduced species that outcompetes native plants and animals, harming the ecosystem.

Killing Frost When temperatures reach around 28 degrees Fahrenheit, it gets cold enough to freeze the water in some plants, killing the ones that are sensitive to cold.

Latitude How far north or south a person or place is from the equator; the equator is at a latitude of 0 degrees, and the North Pole is 90 degrees North.

Legislature The law-making bodies, usually consisting of an upper house (Senate) and a lower house (House of Representatives), in each Midwestern state; these are the officials who make laws pertaining to the environment.

Limestone A sedimentary rock made out of marine animals, such as coral and others; it often preserves fossils within it

Mineral An individual element or combination of elements that is consistent throughout and that has solidified, or crystallized.

Mohs Hardness Scale The relative scale of mineral hardness, from the softest (talc, 1) to the hardest (diamond, 10).

Mutualistic Describes a relationship between two organisms where each one gets something of value or benefit.

Native Describes an animal, plant or organism found naturally in a particular area.

Nonnative Describes an animal, plant, or other organism that isn't naturally found in an area. Note that not all nonnative species are invasive (see above).

Parasite A life form that feeds on or otherwise depends on another life form.

Phenology The study of the seasons and other natural cycles over time.

Rock A combination of two or more minerals.

Scientific Name Because there are so many different plants and animals and other life forms, scientists give each one an official scientific name, usually derived from Latin or Greek and put in *italic text* to make it stand out. Scientific names have two parts: a **genus name,** which is like an organism's last name and which it shares with others, and a **species name,** which is like its first name. So if you want to talk to a scientist about the American Robin, *Turdus migratorius* (yep, that's its real scientific name) is how scientists all around the world would recognize it.

Saprobes Mushrooms that feed on dead or dying material (often wood or plant parts).

Sedimentary A rock that forms as sediment accumulates in layers over long periods of time.

Species Name See **Scientific Name.**

Summer Solstice The longest day of the year, when the earth is pointed most directly at the sun. In the northern hemisphere, the summer solstice occurs in late June.

Temperate Describes an environment where there are long periods (summer!) where the weather is warm.

Toxic Poisonous

Winter Solstice The shortest day of the year; in the northern half of the earth (hemisphere) it occurs in late December when the North Pole is pointed farthest away from the sun.

QUICK QUIZ ANSWERS

Page 5: Springfield, Illinois; Indianapolis, Indiana; Des Moines, Iowa; Topeka, Kansas; Lansing, Michigan; Saint Paul, Minnesota; Jefferson City, Missouri; Lincoln, Nebraska; Bismarck, North Dakota; Columbus, Ohio; Pierre, South Dakota; and Madison, Wisconsin

Page 9: Answer B, Eastern White Pine

Page 11: 1. Basswood 2. Oak 3. Maple

Page 13: Answer C, Wiped out from their original habitat

Page 15: Answer E, All of them

Page 16: Answer B, Norway Pine (Tree of Minnesota)

Page 29: Answer C, Cows

Page 49: 1. Soybeans 2. Corn 3. Sorghum 4. Wheat

Page 79: Petoskey Stone (Michigan), Teredo Petrified Wood (North Dakota), Crinoid (Missouri), and Trilobite (*Isotelus*, Ohio; *Calymena celebra*, Wisconsin)

Page 96: 3. Honeybee (1. is a Calligrapher Fly and 2. is a yellowjacket)

CROSSWORD ANSWERS

Page 86:

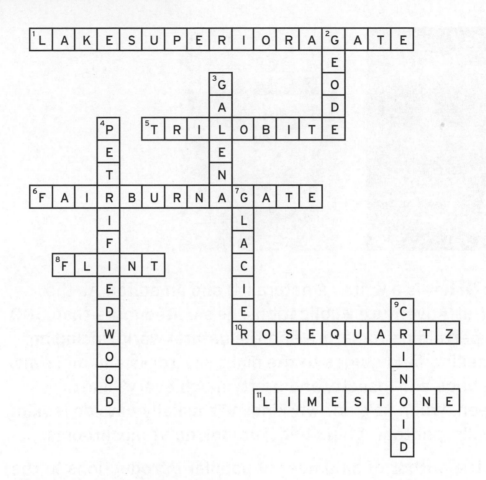

Across:
1. LAKE SUPERIOR AGATE
5. TRILOBITE
6. FAIRBURN AGATE
8. FLINT
10. ROSE QUARTZ
11. LIMESTONE

Down:
2. GEODE
3. GARNET
4. PETRIFIED WOOD
7. GLACIER
9. CRINOID

Page 103:

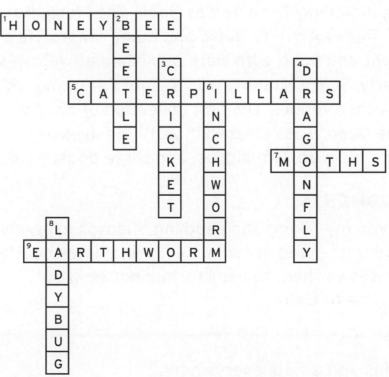

Across:
1. HONEYBEE
5. CATERPILLARS
7. MOTHS
9. EARTHWORM

Down:
2. BEETLE
3. CRICKET
4. DRAGONFLY
6. INCHWORM
8. LADYBUG

ABOUT THE AUTHOR

Brett Ortler is a writer, a naturalist, and an editor. As the editor at Adventure Publications, he's edited more than 300 titles pertaining to nature and the natural world, including best-selling field guides to the night sky, rocks and minerals, birds, bugs and insects, and pretty much everything in between. When he's not working, he's usually outside looking for rocks, photographing bugs, or looking at mushrooms.

He is the author of a number of popular introductions to the natural world, including *The Fireflies Book, The Mosquito Book, Animal Tracks Activity Book,* and many others. He's also an essayist and poet, with work published at websites such as Fatherly, Scary Mommy, and Yahoo! Parenting, as well as many other venues. His first collection of poetry, *Lessons of the Dead,* was released in 2019. He lives in Minnesota with his wife, two kiddos, and three dogs.

ACKNOWLEDGMENTS

Thanks to Oliver, my hiking and paddling buddy; Violet, my backyard bug-hunter; and my wife, Kayli, who hates beetles but somehow allows them to live in a bug house in our kitchen from time to time.

DEDICATION

For curious kids and adults everywhere.

PHOTO CREDITS

A NOTE ABOUT A FEW STATE SYMBOLS

Some of the photos for state symbols were pretty darn hard to find. Instead of just leaving them out, though, I included an image that was as close as I could get (though it's sometimes from a different state or even a different country). –*B.E.O.*

The photos below are copyrighted by their respective photographers. Photos not listed here were taken by Brett Ortler.

Front cover photos: Anastasiia Malinich: Apple Blossom; **Butterfly Hunter:** Monarch Butterfly; **next143:** binoculars; **Paul Reeves Photography:** Garden Spider; **Ronnie Chua:** American Robin; **Steve Mann:** ruler; **Vitaly Korovin:** magnifying glass; **Vitaly Zorkin:** pencil
Back cover photo: Svetlana Foote: Monarch Caterpillar

Page 14 (bison skull), Detroit Public Library, Wikimedia Commons; **Pages 17 and 20** (painted turtle), U.S. Fish & Wildlife Service; **Page 17** (salamander), Sam Stukel, USFWS Mountain-Prairie; **Pages 20 and 75** (greenstone), Dan R. Lynch; **Page 21** (Rusty Patched Bumblebee), Kim Mitchell, USFWS; **Page 22** (mozarkite), Wikipedia User Astynax, public domain; **Pages 23 and 77** (Nebraska Blue Agate), courtesy of Jeff Anderson; jagates.com; **Page 22** (Three-Toed Box Turtle), Wikipedia User Carnopod, public domain; **Page 26** (Black Hills Spruce) USDA-NRCS PLANTS Database; **Page 27** (muskellunge), Eric Engbretson, USFWS; **Pages 27 and 79** (*Calymene celebra*), Wikipedia User Ushakaron; **Page 51** (Hawkeye Point, IA), Jimmy S. Emerson, DVM; **Page 51** (Charles Mound, IN, and Hoosier Hill, IN), Skye Marthaler; **Page 52** (Panorama Point, NE), Wikipedia User Ammodramus, public domain; **Page 52** (Mt. Arvon, MI), Roman Kahler; **Page 53** (White Butte, ND), Wikipedia User Bjr97543, public domain.

Images used under license from Shutterstock: Andriy Kananovych: 80 and 81 (all); **A Kisel:** 9 (maple); **Adam Fichna:** 26 (Ring-Necked Pheasant); **adempercem:** 9 and 18 (oak); **Agnieszka Bacal:** 21 (Common Loon); **Akvals:** 44 and 91 (Dog-Day Cicada); **Al Mueller:** 47 (Bald Eagle); **Alexander Sviridov:** 28 (earthworm); **Anastasiia Malinich:** 20 (Apple Blossom), 34; **Anton_dios:** 17 (dandelion); **ArliftA-toz2205:** 17 (Blue Violet); **arousa:** 11 (American

Basswood leaf); **Aspects and Angles:** 19 (Native Sunflower); **Barbara Storms:** 97 (Sweat Bees); **Beekeepx:** 41 (Sugar Maple flower); **Bob Pool:** 92 (isopod); **Bodan Denysyuk:** 8 (bottom left); **Bogdan Ionescu:** 108 (Chocolate Tube Slime mold); **Bonnie Taylor Barry:** 56 (Northern Cardinal); **Branislav Cerven:** 44 (black raspberries); **Brian A Wolf:** 42 (Baltimore Oriole) and 45 (tamarack); **brizmaker:** 69; **CEW:** 59; **Charles Brutlag:** 42 (Luna Moth); **Cheryl Thomas:** 43 (Monarch Butterfly); **Chris Mursu:** 23 (goldenrod); **Clara Bastian:** 29 (cow); **CLP Media:** 17 (bluegill); **Cynthia Shirk:** 46 (leaves on snow); **Dan Thornberg:** 8 (top); **Daniel Prudek:** honeybee on pp. 19, 22, 23, 26, 27, 88, 96; **David E Haas:** 46 (Sandhill Cranes); **DeStefano:** 29 (Northern Pike); **dibrova:** 24 (American Elm); **Duane Olsen:** 8 (bottom right); **Earl D. Walker:** 27 (granite); **Ed Connor:** 30 (top); **Edgar Lee Espe:** 21 (Showy Lady's Slipper); **Elliot Rusty Harold:** 97 (bumblebee and Carpenter Bee); **EQRoy:** 25 (pawpaw); **Erik Agar:** 91 (Ebony Jewelwing Damselfly); **Ervin-Edward:** 37 (wild strawberries); **Flower_Garden:** 18 (peony); **FotoLot:** 107 (False Morel); **fotolotos:** 37 (lilacs); **FotoRequest:** 55 (Common Loon); **Fredlyfish4:** 51 (Mount Sunflower, KS); **Frode Jacobsen:** 29 (Northern Cardinal); **galitsin:** 92 (worm); **Garrett Gibson:** 28 (starling); **Ghost Bear:** 19 (American Buffalo); **Gints Ivuskans:** 37 (wild raspberries); **godi photo:** 108 (Wolf's Milk Slime); **Gregg Williams:** 18 and 54 (American Goldfinch); **Henrik Larsson:** 88 and 96 (yellowjacket); **High Mountain:** 45 (Jack in the Pulpit); **Hong Vo:** 25 (carnations); **Igor Kovalenko:** 7 (left); **Ilias Strachinis:** 22 and 25 (American Bullfrog); **Jack Bell Photography:** 19, 23 and 24 (Western Meadowlark); **Jacob Boomsma:** 14 (top); **James Opiyo:** 26 (coyote); **Janet M. Kessler:** 20, 27 and 54 (American Robin); **JB Manning:** 32; **Jeff Caverly:** 17, 18, and 25 (Northern Cardinal), 20 (Dwarf Lake Iris); **Jeffrey M. Frank:** 53 (Campbell Hill, OH); **Jennifer Bosvert:** 97 (Mason Bee); **Jennifer

Photo Credits *(continued)*

Princ: (49 (sorghum field); **Jillian Cain Photography:** 68 (osprey nest); **Johnstocker Production:** 28 (German Carp); **Jon Kraft:** 22 (Missouri Mule); **Jovana Kuzmanovic:** 92 (centipede); **Julia Zavalishina:** 105 (Red Fly Agaric); **Karel Bock:** 40 (Skunk Cabbage); **Kimberly Boyles:** 17 (Tully Monster); **Kristi Blokhin:** 68 (Downy Woodpecker); **lecsposure:** 115; **Life Atlas:** 10 (top); **Love Lego:** 20 (mastodon); **Maarten Daams:** 53 (Timm's Hill, WI); **MagicVova:** 42 (wild strawberries); **Marc Bruxelle:** 47 (maple sap bucket); **Marc Goldman:** 28 (House Sparrow); **Marcin Perkowski:** 56 (Ring-Necked Pheasant); **Marco Fine:** Galena on pp. 19, 22, 27, 74, 76, 79; **Martin Fowler:** 28 (Garlic Mustard); **Matt Jeppson:** 19 (Barred Tiger Salamander) and 20 (Brook Trout); **Matt Knoth:** 27 (American Badger); **McCarthy's PhotoWorks:** 84; **Melinda Fawve:** 11 (middle); **Michael Chatt:** 57 (Western Meadowlark); **Michael G McKinne:** 93 (Eastern Tiger Swallowtail); **Michael S. Moncrief:** 108 (Dog Vomit Slime); **Michael Siluk:** 102; **Michael Tatman:** 40 (Red-Winged Blackbird); **Nancy Kennedy:** 27 (Sugar Maple); **naor:** 69 (second from the left); **Nataliia Sokolovskaia:** 33; **Nikolay Kurzenko:** 22 (Flowering Dogwood); **NikolayTsyu:** 42 (lilacs); **Nina B Nichols:** 20 and 75 (Petoskey Stone); **ntv:** 74 (jelinite); **oasisamuel:** 30 (measuring snow); **Ondrej Prosicky:** 37 (Monarch Butterfly); **oticki:** 49 (soybean field); **Paul Reeves Photography:** 36 (American Robin), 92 (Orb-Weaver Spider) and 97 (Mining Bee); **Paul Tessier:** White-Tailed Deer on pp. 17, 20, 23, 25 and 27; **Peter Turner Photography:** 25 (buckeye); **Petr Bonek:** 15 (Prairie Dog); **Philip Bird LRPS CPAGB:** 18 (Tulip Tree); **PhotographyByMK;** 49 (cornfield); **Pictures by Lucy:** geodes on pp. 18 and 73; **Piotr Wawrzyniuk:** walleye on pp. 21 and 26; **poylock19:** 63; **pudiq:** 28 (Glossy Buckthorn); **R Kulawiak:** Eagle Mountain, MN on pp. 50 and 52; **Rabbitti:** 22 (Eastern Bluebird); **Ravshan Mirzaitov:** 42 (Mourning Cloak); **Ricardo Reitmeyer:** 7 (right), 12 (bottom) and 49 (wheat field); **rsev97:** 12 (top); **Rusty Dodson:** 22 (crayfish); **Sam Wagner:** 53 (Black Elk Peak Fire Watch Tower, SD); **Sergey Goruppa:** Channel Catfish on pp. 19, 22, and 23; **stavklem:** 35; **Steve Byland:** 41 (Eastern Bluebird), 55 (Eastern Bluebirds) and 58 (Eastern Bluebird); **Steven Schremp:** 52 (Taum Sauk Mountain, MO); **Stubblefield Photography:** 46 (top); **Sue Smith:** Greenhorn Limestone on pp. 19 and 74; **Sundry Photography:** 120; **Tadashi Okabe:** 44 (soybeans); **Theshutteraffair:** 87; **Timothy R. Nichols:** 97 (Locust Borer); **Tom Reichner:** 62; **Tomasz Klejdysz:** 91 (treehopper); **Vladimir Wrangel:** 24 (Northern Pike); **Wingedbull:** 45 (sumac)

The following (unaltered) images are licensed according to a **Creative Commons Attribution 2.0 Generic (CC BY 2.0) license;** license available at creativecommons.org/licenses/by/2.0:

Page 9 "Tamaracks" by Superior National Forest; original photo via flickr.com/photos/superior nationalforest/6211939680

Page 17 *"Quercus alba"* by Bruce Kirchoff; original photo via flickr.com/photos/bruce kirchoff/20161703291

Pages 22 and 76 *"Synbathocrinus* fossil crinoid (Burlington Limestone, Mississippian; Missouri, USA) 1" by James St. John; original photo via flickr.com /photos/jsjgeology/17383990962

Pages 17 and 73 "Fluorite (mine near Cave-in-Rock, Illinois, USA) 5" by James St. John; original photo via flickr.com/photos/jsjgeology/34398933072

Pages 18 and 73 "Oolitic limestone (Salem Limestone, Middle Mississippian; southern Indiana, USA) 2" by James St. John; original photo via flickr. com/photos/jsjgeology/45243334395

Page 23 "Eastern Cottonwood (*Populus deltoides*)" by Jay Sturner; original photo via commons .wikimedia.org/wiki/Category:Populus_deltoides# /media/File:Eastern_Cottonwood_(Populus _deltoides)_-_Flickr_-_Jay_Sturner_(1).jpg

Page 23 *"Mammuthus imperator maibeni* (Imperial Mammoth) (Late Pleistocene; Karriger Farm, Lincoln County, Nebraska, USA) 12" by James St. John; original photo via flickr.com/photos/jsjgeology-gy/33536816172/

Pages 23 and 77 "Banded Chalcedony (Prairie Agate) (White River Badlands area, western South Dakota, USA) 3" by James St. John; original photo via flickr.com/photos/jsjgeology/15501528177

Pages 24 and 77 *"Teredolites* bivalve borings in fossil conifer wood (Windalia Radiolarite, Lower Cretaceous; Mooka Creek area, Kennedy Ranges, Western Australia)" by James St. John; original photo via flickr.com/photos/jsjgeology/32535818074

Pages 24 and 25 "Convergent Lady Beetle" by Katja Schulz; original photo via flickr.com /photos/treegrow/25504067455

Pages 25 and 78 "Flint (Vanport Flint, Middle Pennsylvanian; Nethers Flint Quarries, Flint Ridge, Ohio, USA) 165" by James St. John; original photo via flickr.com/photos/jsjgeology/41595086272

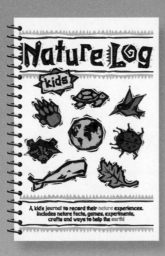
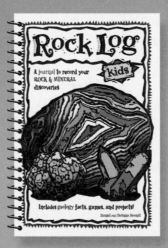
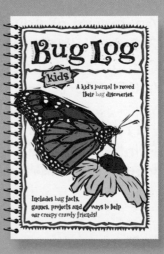

SAFETY NOTE

Nature is wonderful and amazing, and it's certainly nothing to be afraid of, especially if you use common sense and take precautions.

This guide is intended for backyards and green spaces in the Midwest. These places should be pretty safe by definition, but make sure to have an adult with you when you're outside to supervise the activities in this book. And when you're outside, don't reach where you can't see, and be aware of potentially dangerous animals like bees, wasps, ticks, venomous spiders or snakes, and bothersome plants such as poison ivy or poison sumac or oak. There really aren't all that many of these creatures or plants, but if you know they can be found in your area, or if you have allergies (to bees, for instance), it's important to simply be aware that they may be out there.

The best way to stay safe is to keep your distance from wild animals, avoid handling wildlife, and take photos or draw sketches instead. Also, wear gloves, the right clothing for the weather, and sunscreen (as needed), and pay attention to the weather and any potentially unsafe surroundings. Remember: You're responsible for your safety.

An especially important note: Don't use this book to help you identify which wild plants, berries, fruits, or mushrooms are safe to eat. Please leave the berries, fruits, and mushrooms you find for the birds, critters, and the bugs. Instead, get your snacks from the fridge!

10 9 8 7 6 5 4 3 2

Backyard Science & Discovery Workbook: Midwest
Fun Activities and Experiments That Get Kids Outdoors
Copyright © 2021 by Brett Ortler
Published by Adventure Publications
An imprint of AdventureKEEN
310 Garfield Street South
Cambridge, Minnesota 55008
(800) 678-7006
www.adventurepublications.net
All rights reserved
Printed in China
ISBN 978-1-64755-169-8